ALSO BY DAVE BARRY

The Taming of the Screw

Babies and Other Hazards of Sex

Stay Fit and Healthy Until You're Dead

Claw Your Way to the Top

Bad Habits

Dave Barry's Guide to Marriage and/or Sex

Homes and Other Black Holes

Dave Barry's Greatest Hits

Dave Barry Slept Here

Dave Barry Turns Forty

Dave Barry Talks Back

Dave Barry's Only Travel Guide You'll Ever Need

DAVE BARRY
DOES JAPAN

DAVE BARRY

デイブ・バリーが

DOES JAPAN

"日本をする"

DAVE BARRY

FAWCETT COLUMBINE • NEW YORK

A Fawcett Columbine Book
Published by Ballantine Books

Copyright © 1992 by Dave Barry

This edition published by arrangement with Random House, Inc.

GRATEFUL ACKNOWLEDGMENT IS MADE
TO THE FOLLOWING FOR
PERMISSION TO REPRINT PREVIOUSLY PUBLISHED MATERIAL:
EMI Music Publishing: Excerpt from "My Boyfriend's Back" by Richard Gottehrer, Robert Feldman and Gerald Goldstein. Copyright © 1963 by EMI Blackwood Music, Inc. Copyright renewed 1991 by EMI Blackwood Music, Inc. All rights reserved. International copyright secured. Reprinted by permission of EMI Music Publishing.
Famous Music Corporation: Excerpt from "I'm Popeye the Sailor Man" by Sammy Lerner. Copyright 1934 by Famous Music Corporation. Copyright renewed 1961 by Famous Music Corporation. Reprinted by permission.

Library of Congress Catalog Card Number: 93-90032

ISBN: 0-449-90810-0

Cover photo by Bill Wax

Manufactured in the United States of America

First Ballantine Books Edition: October 1993

10 9 8 7 6 5 4 3 2 1

ACKNOWLEDGMENTS

There are a number of people without whom I could not have written this book, but I hope you don't hold that against them. They are all fine people, and they had no idea how it would turn out.

I thank the *Washington Post*'s T. R. Reid, a superb journalist who generously shared his time and knowledge with me. Tom taught me how to say "deliver a homer" in Japanese; you don't soon forget a favor like that. I also thank Tom's colleague Paul Blustein, who had the journalistic courage to risk deportation by getting up in a Tokyo *karaoke* bar with me and singing "My Boyfriend's Back."

I thank Hiroshi Ishikawa of the Japan Press Center for taking my visit seriously, even after seeing the kind of books I write. Without him I'd still be lost in Tokyo, wandering aimlessly in search of my hotel. He's a man of humor and honor, and does his country proud. I also thank two wonderful interpreter/guides: Itsuko Sakai, who took on the near-impossible task of translating Japanese comedians; and Kunio Kadowaki, a wise and tranquil student of life.

Thanks also to my agent, Al Hart, and my editor at Random House, Sam Vaughan. I would describe these men as sage and grizzled veterans of many literary campaigns, except that I have never had the faintest idea what "grizzle" is. This book was largely their idea: They thought it was time I wrote something that involved actually leaving my office. To bring this about, Sam gave me a massive expense account, and Al gave me his lucky talisman to take along. Both of these things were extremely helpful, although I'd have to give the edge to the expense account.

Finally I thank my wife, Beth, a great reporter who is responsible for any genuine facts that appear in this book; and my son, Robby, who made the ultimate sacrifice for this book: *three whole weeks* without real pizza.

CONTENTS

DAVE BARRY
DOES JAPAN

INTRODUCTION

*The Background
of This Book:
TV Violence*

My first impressions of the Japanese came from watching them act like raving homicidal maniacs on television. This was in 1953, when I was six, and we got our first TV set, one of those comical old models with a teensy screen embedded in a wooden cabinet roughly the size of the house where Lincoln was born. Many of the programs I watched on that little screen involved homicidal maniacs. If I had to summarize the important early lesson I learned from TV, it would be: "Watch out—the world is full of people who want to kill you!"[1] The western shows, for example, were infested with bad men who did nothing but grow chin stubble and ride around shooting people. Your average hero cowboy, such as Gene Autry or the Cisco Kid, could not ride his horse twenty feet without getting ambushed by bad guys packing six-guns that could shoot 17 million bullets without reloading.

Fortunately the bad guys had the tactical intelligence of a waffle iron, so the hero was able to outsmart them by ducking behind some rocks, then putting his hat on a stick and holding it up. The bad guys—who never learned, no matter how many times this trick was played on them—were fooled into thinking that the hat contained the good guy's actual head, so they'd shoot all 17 million bullets, each of which would ricochet off the rocks with a loud *chinngggg*. (Forget erosion: The main reason why the western landscape is so rugged is that bad guys ricocheted so many bullets off it.)

Even outer space had maniacs. I learned this from a show called *Captain Video*, featuring a man named, oddly, Captain Video, a space pioneer in charge of an extremely low-budget spaceship that

---

[1] It turns out that this is probably true.

appeared to be made from materials that you might find around a TV studio. For example, the device he used for communicating back to the Earth was obviously a regular telephone; Captain Video held the handset as though it were a microphone and talked into the listening end.

While pioneering around the universe, Captain Video kept running into homicidal space aliens with Russian accents. In my favorite episode, an alien invented a robot named—get ready for a clever robot name—Tobor, who looked a lot like a man wearing cardboard boxes covered with Reynolds Wrap. In the dramatic final scene, the villain orders Tobor to get Captain Video.

"Attack, Tobor!" says the villain, and Tobor lumbers toward Captain Video. Things look very bad, but suddenly, at the last instant, with Tobor only inches away, Captain Video has an idea—a crazy idea, but one that *just might work.*

"Go back, Tobor!" he says.

And Tobor, who clearly was not in the gifted program at robot school, *turns around* and starts lumbering toward the villain.

"Attack, Tobor!" says the villain, and Tobor once again goes into reverse lumber.

"Go back, Tobor!" says the captain, who was probably up all night memorizing his lines.

For most of the episode Tobor goes back and forth until finally he breaks down, thus ending the threat, because you know how difficult it is to get a robot serviced in space.

But the most maniacal of all the maniacs I watched on TV were the Japanese soldiers in the World War II movies. The German soldiers were also homicidal, but they weren't *crazy*. Whereas the Japanese—always sensitively referred to as "Japs"—were completely out of their minds. They'd crash their planes on you and leap out of palm trees on your head and just generally swarm at you like some species of giant suicidal shrieking, sword-waving, spittle-emitting insect. Total wackmobiles.

You could always tell when the Japanese were about to appear because brass instruments on the sound track would play an ominous, Oriental-sounding musical chord. A group of GIs would be walking through the jungle, nervous but still making spunky American wisecracks, and suddenly the sound track would go:

BWAAAAAAAAAMP

And right away you knew there were Japs in the trees, ready to pounce.

Or a U.S. Navy ship would be motoring along, and the lookout would put his binoculars to his eyes, and

BWAAAAAAAAAMP

there would be a Jap destroyer. Probably one of the major reasons why the Japanese lost the war is that the sound track kept giving their position away.

But they were tough. They fought like crazy, and they would do anything to win, including taunt the Americans in an unsportsmanlike fashion

("Hey! GI Joe!") from their jungle hiding places. If they captured one of our guys their leader always turned out to have a UCLA education, which he then—talk about ingratitude—turned against us. *("American! Terr me the rocation of yoah headquatah! I see you suppry I speak Engrish so werr.")*

The point is that my initial impression of the Japanese was not favorable. Fortunately, as I grew older my intellectual horizons broadened, and I no longer received information about the outside world exclusively from television; I also started going to horror movies. From these I learned that Japan was not just a weird foreign country that had tried to kill us; it was also a weird foreign country that was for some reason under almost constant attack by giant mutated creatures. Godzilla was the most famous one, of course, but there were also hyperthyroid pterodactyls, spiders, etc., all of which regularly barged into Tokyo and committed acts of mass destruction. I imagine this eventually became so commonplace that Japanese TV weathermen included it in their forecasts. ("Partly cloudy this afternoon, with a sixty percent chance that Tokyo will be leveled by immense radioactive worms.")

These movies always had a scene wherein the creature, striding through the streets, would knock over a crowded commuter train. It must have been hell being a Tokyo commuter in those days. You'd arrive at work two hours late, and try to explain to your boss that your train had been flung into the harbor by an irate praying mantis the size of Belgium, and he'd say, "What, *again?*"

My only other contact with Japan was through products made there, mostly cheap toys that my father would sometimes bring home for me. These did not survive long in the harsh environment of my room. I'd get a little friction-motor car, and I'd rev it up to about 20,000 rpm and set it loose, and it would hit the wall and—*sproing!*—disintegrate into dozens of tiny car parts. It would have been more efficient if my dad, instead of going to all the trouble of lugging these toys home, had just smashed them with a hammer right at the toy store.

Automobiles: Us

Back then, of course, we thought *all* Japanese products were cheap. How could the Japanese make good products, given the time they spent fleeing from Godzilla? The suggestion that Japan could make *real* cars would have been laughable. *Real* cars were made here in America: Fords, Chevys, Plymouths. These were large chunks of Detroit iron—cars that had the size, weight, and handling characteristics of aircraft carriers but worse fuel efficiency; cars with huge engines and vast backseats that a person could get pregnant in without undue contortion and big round dashboard clocks that never moved. (I think there was a quality control inspector at the end of every auto-assembly line to check the clocks; if he found one that worked, he sent the car back.)

Back then you formed a family loyalty to a brand. If your parents were Ford people, you were a Ford person, and every few years you traded your Ford in for another Ford. It was like a religion. When I was a student at Pleasantville High School[2] in the sixties, the major lunchtime activity for a large group of boys—the industrial arts students, or "hoods," for short—was to stand on a corner just off school property, wearing tight black pants that stopped at midcalf, smoking unfiltered Camel cigarettes, spitting frequently, and holding long scholarly debates concerning the issue of Ford versus Chevy:

FORD GUY: Ain't no [bad word] *way* that any [bad word] piece of Chevy [bad word] is gonna beat a 497 with dual overhauled quad thrusted cams!
CHEVY GUY: Oh yeah?
(They fight.)

Actually, I don't think there were many important mechanical differences among American cars back then. The big difference was styling. Every year the manufacturers would come out with

---

[2] Team name: The Panthers.

new models featuring more chrome and bigger fins, in a fierce competition to see who could produce the ugliest car. The winner was Chrysler, which in the late fifties came out with a model that had a set of fins tall enough to menace commercial aviation. Any given one of these fins contained sufficient sheet metal to house all the poor families in Mexico City. This car looked like Captain Video's rocket ship. But people bought it, because it was a big, solid American car, and, by God, Americans knew how to make a car.

My first inkling that Japan might be able to make a vehicle that was not powered by a friction motor came in the late sixties, when I was in college, and my friend Buzz Burger bought a Honda motorcycle. It had a hilarious, incomprehensible owner's manual that appeared to have been translated from Japanese to English by somebody who spoke only Swahili. It was full of statements like:

WARNING! To take and put the earth wire not having a smart holding, a fatal eventuality may incur.

We got a lot of entertainment reading aloud from this manual when we were supposed to be studying. Those wacky Japanese! Thinking they could put out an owner's manual! We couldn't help but notice, however, that it was a really *good* motorcycle. To start other motorcycles, especially in cold weather, you had to mess around with various adjustments, then spend twenty minutes or so jumping up and down on the kick-starter while cursing. Whereas to start Buzz's Honda, you just turned the key and pressed a button, and *purrrrrr* it was running nice and smooth.

So, we figured, OK, maybe they could make a motorcycle. Also we were starting to hear some good things about radios made by a company called Sony. But that certainly didn't mean that there was any reason for us to be concerned about America losing its

BWAAAAAAAAAMP

Hey! What was that sound? Probably nothing, we figured. We didn't think about it; we were occupied with being Leaders of the Free World, which meant building a Great Society *plus* fighting a war in Vietnam *plus* defending all of Western Europe from the Soviet Menace *plus* building enough nuclear weapons to vaporize the entire planet 173 times *plus* sending an endless procession of men with nicknames like "Doke" to the Moon. We didn't have *time* to be worrying about what Japan was up to. We were *busy*.

Automobiles: Them

Then, in the seventies, we suddenly ran out of oil.[3] There were huge lines of cars at the gas stations,

---

[3] I *still* don't really know why this happened, do you? Maybe we just forgot to reorder.

and people were actually shooting each other in disputes about line-butting. It was a scary time.[4] A lot of people started thinking that maybe they should buy small, fuel-efficient cars. And guess who was making them?

BWAAAAAAAAAMP

That's right. The wacky little maniacs were now making cars, with comical names like Toyota. They didn't *look* very sharp—in fact, they looked like large versions of the friction-motor cars I used to smash into my wall—but they ran pretty well, and they got good mileage, and they were dependable and cheap. More and more people started buying them.

Automobiles: Us

At first the American auto manufacturers resisted making small cars for aesthetic reasons: Smaller cars sell for less money. But finally, feeling the pinch from foreign competition, the U.S. auto makers decided that, OK, they would make small cars. But not just *any* small cars: No, they would make *really bad* small cars. The shrewd marketing strategy here was that people would buy these cars, realize how crappy they were, and go back to aircraft carriers. This

---

[4] As opposed to today, when we shoot each other in disputes about parking spaces.

strategy resulted in cars such as the Ford Pinto, the Chevrolet Vega, and the American Motors Gremlin—cars that were apparently designed during office Christmas parties by drunken mail-room employees drawing on napkins; cars that frequently disintegrated *while they were still on the assembly line.*

I know what I'm talking about here. In 1971 I purchased a Vega, which I believe was manufactured entirely out of compressed rust. Moments after I bought it, the body began developing little holes, which turned into bigger holes, until the Vega looked like an educational demonstration X-ray car, with most of its body removed so that interested onlookers could examine its working parts. Except that it hardly *had* any working parts. It did have a recurring ignition problem, so the only way I could get it running was to raise the hood and use a screwdriver to connect two metal things, which would cause sparks to go shooting around the engine compartment and sometimes also cause the engine to actually start, but frequently not. I spent many hours waiting for tow trucks, idly picking large rust flakes off the fender and listening to parts fall off. Parts were always falling off the Vega. If I couldn't remember where I'd left it in a parking lot, I'd just stand still for a moment, listening, and—*clang*—there would be the familiar sound of the Vega jettisoning, say, a shock absorber.

And the Vega wasn't even the worst of the small American cars. The Pinto sometimes *ex-*

ploded. ("Where'd we park, Marge?" *BOOM.* "Over there!") But these were the vehicles Detroit was offering us. And so, more and more, we bought from the Japanese, whose cars were growing less comical-looking all the time. Finally the U.S. manufacturers realized that, if they were going to win this fight, they'd have to employ something other than the Really Bad Car strategy. So, showing the kind of spunky, independent, "can-do" pioneer spirit that made America the self-reliant nation it is, they went whining to the government for help. Industry leaders like Lee "Air Bag" Iacocca argued that Americans needed import restrictions to protect them from the threat of cheaper and better Japanese cars.

Other Stuff: Them

But it was too late. American consumers had discovered that they *really liked* Japanese products. And not just cars, either. You walked into any home-electronics store and

BWAAAAAAAAAMP

you were surrounded by new and wondrously clever made-in-Japan devices that were *crying out* to become a part of your life-style. *("Hey! GI Joe! You rike Mitsubishi VCR, yes?")*

Also there were cameras and skis and guitars and pianos, all of them well made. The Japanese were sending freighters full of products over to us, and we were sending freighters full of money back. And then they were starting to use that money to purchase things that we had always thought of as unalterably, uniquely *American,* such as Hawaii. We didn't like this, but we kept buying their products. We had come to just *assume* that anything made in Japan was better than anything we could make.

Of course, there was a lot of hand-wringing about this. We asked ourselves: What *happened* to us? Why can't *we* make VCRs? It seemed as though every week the newspaper had yet another article about yet another study showing that American children who were graduating from high school scored lower on standardized academic tests than Japanese children who were still in the womb.

We wondered. And worried. Are we really *stupider* than they are? Can it be that we're *inferior* to the little banzai wackmobiles? This is a very difficult concept for Americans, long the butt-kickers of the world, to even think about. The irony is, we spent all those years in the life-or-death Cold War Struggle against the Evil Soviet Menace, and we finally achieved victory so total that by 1991, the only remaining Soviet menace was that you might get crushed under a statue of Lenin being toppled by a crowd of Latvians wearing Guess jeans. This should have been a time for us to pour champagne on our heads and shout "We're number one!" and hold street celebrations culminating in widespread arrests and some looting, but instead we looked around and secretly speculated: Are we really number one? Do we *feel* like we're number one, with our lousy schools and our wasted cities and our pandering slimeball "leaders" in Washington and our endless whining lawsuits caused by a ratio of roughly four lawyers for every human and all our multiskillion-dollar weapons systems protecting us from *what?* From freighters filled with Infinitis ordered by orthodontists in Connecticut?

So we thought: Maybe we're not number one after all. And we looked at the Japanese, with their booming economy and their high literacy rate and their low crime rate and their tourists showing up all over the world wearing designer clothes that we can't afford and spending bales of money in exclusive stores that we don't even dare walk into, and they *ticked us off.* I mean, we beat them in the war, right? We *invented* the automobile, right? We are, on average, taller, right? Who the hell do they think they are?

Oh, there's a lot of anger. Every now and then you see a news story about a group of American workers, usually assisted by a member of Congress, demonstrating their concern over Japanese imports by smashing the hell out of a Japanese radio with a sledgehammer. This is, of course, an extremely effective way to reduce Japanese imports, the only teensy little flaw being that it's stupid, because in order to smash a Japanese radio, you have to import it. Some smart Japanese company is probably

doing a brisk business over here, selling radios that
are specially designed to smash in a dramatic and
photogenic manner. This company also supplies
the sledgehammer, and perhaps even the member
of Congress.

But never mind the economic logic. The point
is that there's a lot of hostility and mistrust on both
sides, and as Japan has grown stronger, the rela-
tionship between the two countries has gotten
worse. There was even a best-selling book not long
ago called *The Coming War with Japan,* although
I hate to think that we'd be foolish enough to go to
war with Japan, because there's always the terrible
danger that we'd win again.

But the mere fact that we can even *think* about
another war shows how bad things have gotten,
and how important it is for us to try to improve
understanding between these two great nations.
And that's why I wrote this book: to try, in some
small way, to make this world a better place for
people everywhere, and for the generations to
come.

I'm lying, of course. I wrote this book because
I thought a trip to Japan might be pretty funny,
especially since Random House had generously
agreed to pay for the whole thing. This was a major
factor, because I had heard that prices were pretty
high in Japan. People who'd been there were always telling me horror stories. "Oh, yes," they'd
say. "In Tokyo, Frank ordered two eggs over medium and the bill came to $16,500, plus $312 for the

parsley sprig, and he wound up having to sell both of his corneas."

So in the summer of 1991 I filled several large suitcases with traveler's checks and went to Japan with my wife, Beth, and my ten-year-old son, Robert. We spent three weeks bumbling around in a disoriented, uncomprehending manner, The Three Cultural Stooges, because it turns out that Japan is an *extremely* foreign country, where you can never be sure whether the sign on the door you're about to open says:

RESTAURANT

or:

ENTER HERE FOR EXPRESS VASECTOMY SERVICE.

This book is an account of that trip. Please don't misunderstand me: I don't claim to have become an expert on Japan in three weeks. The Japanese culture is thousands of years old; to truly grasp its incredible complexity and infinite subtle nuance, you'd need at least a month.

Ha-ha! Just kidding. I don't know if an outsider can ever really understand Japan, but I know we never came close. When I arrived there, my major objectives immediately changed from things like "try to determine attitude of average salaried worker toward government industrial policy" to things like "try to find food without suckers on it."

So this book is not authoritative. If you want authoritative, go buy a real book. This book is just a highly subjective account of our trip, with a lot of personal impressions, some of which may well have been influenced by beer, which by the way is another thing they do better than we do. In fact, they do quite a few things better than we do, and I'm not just talking about cars and radios. But it also turns out that we are *way* ahead of them in important areas, such as pizza.

My most important finding, however, does not involve the differences between us and Japan; it involves the similarities. Because despite the gulf, physical and cultural, between the United States and Japan, both societies are, in the end, made up of people, and people everywhere—when you strip away their superficial differences—are crazy.

FAILING TO LEARN JAPANESE IN ONLY FIVE MINUTES

Or: "Very Much Good Morning, Sir!"

The way I attempted to learn Japanese was by reading a book called *Japanese at a Glance* in the plane from San Francisco to Tokyo. This is not the method recommended by experts. The method recommended by experts is to be born as a Japanese baby and raised by a Japanese family, in Japan.

20

And even then it's not easy. Learning to *speak* Japanese isn't so bad,[1] but learning to *read* it is insanely difficult. Start with the fact that, for some malevolent reason, the Japanese use *four different systems,* which are often intermixed, in addition to characters sometimes arranged vertically, in which case you read right to left, but sometimes arranged horizontally, in which case you read left to right. (I might have gotten some of this wrong, but, trust me, there's no way you'd be able to tell.) Also sometimes there's a mixture of horizontal and vertical writing, using several different character systems.

That's not the hard part. The hard part is that the major Japanese writing system consists of— why not?—*Chinese* characters, which represent words, not sounds. So for each word, you need a different character, which means to be even moderately literate you have to memorize thousands and thousands of characters. This wouldn't be so bad if the characters looked like what they're supposed to represent. For example, if the character for "dog" looked like this:

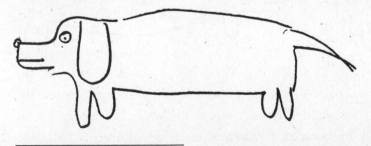

---

[1] Not that *I* ever came close.

21

And "bird" looked like this:

And "politician" looked like this:

Then you could form a simple sentence like this:

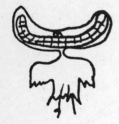 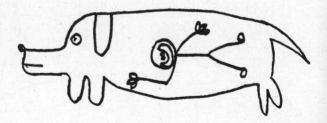

And even a child would easily understand the meaning.[2] But the Japanese/Chinese characters don't look anything like the concepts they're supposed to represent. They all look approximately like this:

And *every one of those marks is important.* If you put one teensy little line in there wrong, you could change the entire meaning of the character, from something like "man holding broom" to "sex with ostriches."

Sometimes it seems as though the whole point of the Japanese writing system is to keep non-Japanese people from understanding what the hell is going on. The only Westerner I met in Japan who had actually learned to read Chinese/Japanese characters was Tom Reid, who works for the *Washington Post.* He was always trying to explain it to me. He'd write down something that looked like this:

---

[2] "The bird smiled when the dog ate the politician."

Then he'd say, "OK, this character means 'library infested with vermin.' See, this line here"—*here he points to a line that appears identical to all the other lines*—"looks like a tree root, right? And books are the *root* of knowledge, right? Get it? And this line"—*he points to another random line*—looks like the whisker of a rat, right? You see it, right? *RIGHT?*"

I'd always say that yes, I thought I saw it, although what I really thought was that Tom had spent too many hours studying rats' whiskers.

So I never even tried to learn the written language. I sincerely did intend to learn to speak some Japanese before we went over there, but, because of a lot of other things I had to do to prepare for the trip,[3] it turned out that the only concrete linguistic effort I made was to go with my wife and son to a Benihana of Tokyo restaurant in Miami. We thought maybe we could pick up some useful

---

[3] Such as signing traveler's checks for about three straight days.

phrases from the waiter, who came out and pre- pared our steak right in front of us by assaulting it violently with sharp implements and hurling it around the griddle, as though concerned that it might suddenly come to life and attack the pa- trons. But it turned out that he was Cuban, and the only Japanese expression he knew was the sound you make when you strike a potentially dangerous steak.[4]

So I ended up attempting to learn Japanese on the flight over. I had plenty of time, because flying from the United States to Tokyo takes approxi- mately as long as law school. But the flight is not so bad when you do it the way we did it, namely, first class on Japan Air Lines, with Random House pay- ing for it. This is definitely the way you should do it, if you ever go to Japan. Just tell your travel professional, "I'd like to fly first class, and send the bill to Random House." Don't mention my name.

We've flown long distances before, but it was always in coach class—thousands of passengers jammed together, thigh-to-thigh, their elbows bruised and bleeding from hours of dueling for position on armrests the width of a number two pencil; homeless people living in the overhead-bag- gage compartments; cattle-prod-carrying flight at- tendants offering the Battle of the Dinner Entree Options, featuring Martian Meat versus Paleolithic

---

[4] "HARGGHH!"

Pasta; long Soviet-style lines of people waiting to use the three lavatories, two of which are out of order and the third of which has run out of toilet paper, leaving the traveler with no choice but to use in-flight magazine articles with titles like "The Birdbaths of Denmark."

First class on Japan Air Lines is not like this. Your seat alone is larger than the original Wright Brothers aircraft, and it reclines into essentially a bed, and while you're lying there, feeling like one of the more degenerate Roman emperors, the cabin attendants—there seem to be about fifteen of them—constantly come around to give you gourmet dinners, wines, cheeses, desserts, more wines, more dinners, more cheeses, more desserts, more wines, until you, personally, account for about a third of the plane's total gross weight. Also they shower you with complimentary items for you to keep: slippers, headphones, eye masks, ear plugs, toiletry kits, robes, stationery sets—they keep producing these things, and they continue feeding you, until after several hours you're an enormous bloated blob of reclining flesh, buried under a mound of complimentary gift items, and *still* they want to know what else they can do for you. You get the feeling that they'd be thrilled to do your federal tax returns, or give you an on-board facelift. Or that you could casually mention that you have always wanted to see a fjord, and instantly the captain would change course for Norway.

Speaking of the captain, the only disconcerting event that occurred on the flight—and I'm still not totally certain that it *did* occur—came in the middle of the night, when most of the passengers were sleeping, and I was drinking a beer and thinking very seriously about starting to read *Japanese at a Glance,* and one of the cabin attendants came around and asked me and my son, Robby, who was also still awake,[5] if we'd like to see the cockpit. We said sure, and we lurched out of our seats and climbed up a little curved stairway and went past what I believe was an armed guard into the cockpit, where some alert-looking men with excellent posture were frowning thoughtfully at about 650,000,-000,000,000,000,000,000 instruments.

One of the men, the navigator, I think, pointed out the window at some islands off to the right.

"Aleutian Islands," he said.

"Robby," I said, translating, "those are the Aleutian Islands."

"Huh," said Robby.

"Huh," I explained to the navigator.

"Yes," he said.

As we were leaving, the cabin attendant, a soft-spoken, deferential woman, turned to me, smiling, and, in a jocular tone of voice, said—I am almost positive this is what she said, although

---

[5] He is *always* awake. I'm talking about since *birth*.

maybe it was the late hour and the wine—"When we pass by the Aleutians, we will get shot down by the Russians."

WHAT? is what I thought.

"Ha-ha!" is what I said, to show that my sense of humor is as good as the next first-class passenger's.

As it happened, we never did get shot down, but thanks to the stimulating first-class conversation, before I fell asleep I was able to devote nearly an hour to the study of the Japanese language. My ultimate goal was to learn how to say "I do not speak Japanese" in fluent Japanese, but I decided to start with "Thank you." According to *Japanese at a Glance,* the way you say this is:

DOH-moh ah-REE-gah-toh

For some reason—again, it could have been the wine—I found this almost impossible to remember. I tried practicing on the cabin attendants, who continued to come around every few minutes with complimentary items.

"DI-moh ah-bli-GA-toh," I would say.

Or: "DE-mi AL-le-GRET-oh."

Or: "DA-moh o-RE-ga-noh."

All of these seemed to work pretty well, but I think the cabin attendants were just being polite. I

was worried about how I'd do with regular Japa-

nese civilians, especially in light of the following
stern warning from *Japanese at a Glance:*

> Take long vowels seriously; pronouncing a long
> vowel incorrectly can result in a different word,
> or even an unintelligible one.

So I tried hard to take my long vowels seriously. The last thing I wanted was to try to thank
a bellhop and instead, because of a vowel problem,
ask for his hand in marriage. After a solid hour I
was still not at all confident in my "Thank you,"
and most of the other phrases in *Japanese at a
Glance* were even worse. It was as if they had been
cranked out by the Random Syllable Generator.
The harder I tried to concentrate, the more confusing the phrases became, until they all looked like
this:

HELLO (formal): Wa-SO-hah-na-GO-ma-na-SO-la-ti-
DOH
HELLO (informal): Hah-to-RAH-ma-ka-NYAH-nyah-
nyah
HELLO (during rain): KO-rah-na-mah-NAY-ah-MOO-
baaaaa

I fell asleep babbling politely and dreamed
about the Russians.

The result of this language-training program
was that I arrived in Tokyo speaking Japanese at

29

essentially the same fluency level as cement. I never did get much better while we were there. The only word I became really good at saying was "beer," which is pronounced "bee-roo," unless you want a big beer, in which case it is pronounced "BIG bee-roo." I semimastered a few other Japanese words, but I tended to use them randomly. To give you a true example: One evening a hotel waiter brought me a beer; I thanked him in Japanese, and he bowed politely and went away, at which point my son observed that what I had actually said to the waiter was "Very much good morning, sir."

Fortunately, my inability to learn Japanese was not much of a problem, thanks to a little pocket-sized reference card that came with *Japanese at a Glance,* entitled THE 32 MOST USEFUL JAPANESE PHRASES. I carried this card everywhere. On the left-hand side it listed 32 English phrases, such as "Do you speak English?"; "I'm lost"; "Where's the rest room?"; etc. On the right-hand side, the card told you how to pronounce these phrases in Japanese. Here, for example, with no exaggeration, is how you're supposed to pronounce "I'm lost":

Mee-chee nee, mah-YOHT-teh shee-mah-ee-mah-shtah

Even reading from this card, it would probably take me fifteen minutes to pronounce this successfully, and I'm not sure how much good it would do me. Let's say I actually managed to say to a

Japanese person, "Mee-chee nee, mah-YOHT-teh shee-mah-ee-mah-shtah." The Japanese person would probably respond with something like, "na-go-wah-ME-yoh-nah-mah-TSOY-yah-ska-wo-mah," meaning "I see." And then I'd need *another* phrase, requiring another fifteen minutes to pronounce. In terms of time management, it seemed more efficient simply to remain lost, which is pretty much what we did for the whole three weeks.

This is not to say that THE 32 MOST USEFUL JAPANESE PHRASES was not helpful. *Au contraire.*[6] I found the card to be invaluable, once I grasped how to use it. The trick was to *ignore the right-hand, or Japanese, side.* Very few Japanese persons understood me when I attempted to pronounce useful phrases in Japanese. But I did pretty well when I read the *left* side of the card very slowly. I'd say:

Where-is-the-REST-room?

And almost always somebody would understand well enough to point me in the right direction. (This was not always a good thing, because the Japanese concept of "toilet" is basically the same as our concept of "a hole in the floor that somebody forgot to put a toilet on top of."[7])

My point is that many Japanese people know

---

[6] Or, as the Japanese say, "Ee-gah-wo-nah-TKSKA-ka-do-ma-oo-mau-mau."

[7] More on this important subject later.

a little English. But it's often *very* little. Japan is not like, for example, Germany, where everybody seems to speak English better than the average U.S. congressperson. In Japan, you will often find yourself in situations where nobody speaks any English. And the weird thing is, English pops up *everywhere* in Japan. You constantly see signs and advertisements with English words in them, and you constantly hear American rock music being played in stores and restaurants. But to the Japanese, the English doesn't seem to *mean* anything. It's there purely for decorative purposes, like a hood ornament, or a SPEED LIMIT 55 sign.

This can be frustrating. I remember being in a Kentucky Fried Chicken restaurant[8] in a small town called Beppu, trying to communicate the concept of "ketchup" to the young man behind the counter, who, like virtually every other Japanese person we met, was extremely polite and diligent. He was trying hard to understand me, frowning with intense concentration as I used the Official United Nations International Gesture for "ketchup," which is to pound the bottom of an upside-down imaginary ketchup bottle while saying

Ketchup? Ketchup? Ketchup?

---

[8] Of *course* they have Kentucky Fried Chicken restaurants. Don't be an idiot.

like a person with a hiccups-related nerve disorder. But I wasn't getting through, so the young man called two young women over, and all three of them solemnly watched me repeat

Ketchup? Ketchup? Ketchup?

for a while longer, none of them saying a word, and all the while the store's music system was playing:

There she was, just a-walkin' down the street
Singin' do-wah diddy diddy dum diddy-do

And I wanted to scream, HOW CAN YOU NOT UNDERSTAND ENGLISH WHEN ALL DAY LONG YOU LISTEN TO "DO-WAH DIDDY DIDDY DUM DIDDY DO"??
The answer is that they don't really care what the words say; they just like the sound. It's the same with printed English words. The Japanese don't care what they mean; they just like the way they look. They especially like clothes imprinted with English words, words that often seem to be chosen at random. This results in a phenomenon that has vastly amused thousands of English-speaking visitors: the unintentionally hilarious T-shirt. Anybody who has spent any time in Japan can give you examples. Tom Reid, of the *Washington Post,* told me that he once covered a ceremony where a Japanese high-school student received a very prestigious science award; the student accepted the award

wearing a T-shirt that said SNOT HOUSE. I once saw an attractive, stroller-pushing young mother wearing heels, a nice skirt, and a blouse imprinted with CIRCUIT BEAVER.

Here are just a few of the other fascinating statements we saw on T-shirts, and as I am fond of saying when reporting facts, I am not making this up:

I AM PLUMP MARY.
WE'RE BONE NOB. WE'RE HAPPY OUR ORIGINAL DANCE.
NURSE MENTALITY
WE HOPE TO ALWAYS HAVE AN OPEN
A SOUVENIR GOODS MAKE US HAPPY ANYTIME. DON'T YOU
THINK SO?
BONERACTIVE WEAR

We also saw signs that told us where we could find:

VENOM FOOD AND BAR[9]
LIQUOR BY THE GRASS OR IN COOKTAIL
JIVE COFFEE
FASHION VS. HAIR

On a cigarette-vending machine in Kyoto, we found the following quotations, with no further explanation:

---

[9] This establishment was in a section of Tokyo called Roppongi, whose motto is: "A High Touch Town."

"It is common practice over there to offer each other a cigarette as daily greetings."

"So I heard. Cigarettes are offered to the other to express friendliness and affection."

The important lesson for the English-speaking visitor to learn from all this is that, again, in Japan, English words do not necessarily mean anything. Adding to the confusion is the fact that, even when English words DO mean something, it may not be what you think. The Japanese are not big on saying things directly. Another way of putting this: Compared with the Japanese, the average American displays in communication all the subtlety of Harpo hitting Zeppo with a dead chicken. The Japanese tend to communicate via nuance and euphemism, often leaving important things unsaid; whereas Americans tend to think they're being subtle when they refrain from grabbing the listener by the shirt.

This difference in approach often leads to misunderstandings between the two cultures. One of the biggest problems—all the guidebooks warn you about this—is that the Japanese are extremely reluctant to come right out and say no, a word they generally regard as impolite. My wife, Beth, learned this before we even got to Japan, when she was making airplane and hotel arrangements through a Japanese travel agent. Beth, who is an extremely straight-ahead type of communicator, was having a hell of a time, because she kept having conversations like this:

35

BETH: . . . and then we want to take a plane from Point A to Point B.

TRAVEL AGENT: I see. You want to take a plane?

BETH: Yes.

TRAVEL AGENT: From Point A?

BETH: Yes.

TRAVEL AGENT: To Point B?

BETH: Yes.

TRAVEL AGENT: Ah.

BETH: Can we do that?

TRAVEL AGENT: Perhaps you would prefer to take a train.

BETH: No, we would prefer to take a plane.

TRAVEL AGENT: Ah-hah. You would prefer to take a plane?

BETH: Yes. A plane.

TRAVEL AGENT: I see. From Point A?

And so it would go, with arrangement after arrangement. Inevitably, by the time Beth got off the phone, she was a raving madwoman.

"What is the PROBLEM??" she would shout, causing the dogs to crawl around on their stomachs (in case they had done something wrong). "Why can't these people COMMUNI-CATE???"

The answer, of course, is that the travel agent was communicating. A person familiar with the Japanese culture would recognize instantly that the agent was virtually screaming, "THERE IS NO PLANE, YOU ZITBRAIN!"

To the best of my knowledge, in all the time
we traveled around Japan, nobody ever told us we
couldn't do anything, although it turned out that
there were numerous things we couldn't do. Life
became easier for us once we learned to interpret
certain key phrases, which I'll summarize in this
convenient table:

ENGLISH STATEMENT MADE BY JAPANESE PERSON	ACTUAL MEANING IN AMERICAN
I see.	No.
Ah.	No.
Ah-hah.	No.
Yes.	No.
That is difficult.	That is completely impossible.
That is very interesting.	That is the stupidest thing I ever heard.
We still study your proposal.	We will feed your proposal to a goat.

Before we left for Japan, I had several phone
conversations with Hiroshi Ishikawa of the Foreign
Press Center in Tokyo, who was of great help in
arranging interviews and interpreters, and whom I
now consider a friend. In our first conversation, we
had this exchange:

HIROSHI: You are going to be here three weeks?

ME: Yes.

HIROSHI: I see. And you are going to write a book?

ME: Yes.

HIROSHI: I see. And you expect to gather enough material in three weeks to write a book?

ME: Well, it's not going to be a *good* book. *(Pause for laughter.)*

HIROSHI: I see.

After we got to Japan, I realized that Hiroshi had been expressing vast skepticism about the whole idea, but fortunately I was oblivious to this at the time. I'm sure I was oblivious to the true meaning of almost everything everybody said to me over there. I frankly wonder how Americans and Japanese ever communicate with each other about *anything*. According to the guidebooks, when two Japanese businessmen meet, they tend to be very formal, and each man tends to be self-effacing and apologetic, often for no apparent reason:

FIRST BUSINESSMAN: Hello, sir.

SECOND BUSINESSMAN: Hello, sir.

FIRST BUSINESSMAN: I am sorry.

SECOND BUSINESSMAN: I am extremely sorry.

FIRST BUSINESSMAN: I cannot stand myself.

SECOND BUSINESSMAN: I am swamp scum.

FIRST BUSINESSMAN: I am toenail dirt.

SECOND BUSINESSMAN: I should be put to death.

Only after a great deal of this do they get down to business. Contrast this with a typical dialogue between American businessmen:

FIRST BUSINESSMAN: Bob!

SECOND BUSINESSMAN: Ed!

FIRST BUSINESSMAN: How they hangin'?

SECOND BUSINESSMAN: One lower than the other!

FIRST BUSINESSMAN: Har!

SECOND BUSINESSMAN: Listen, about those R-243-J's, the best we can do for you is $3.80 a unit.

FIRST BUSINESSMAN: My ass, Bob.

SECOND BUSINESSMAN: Har!

No, subtlety and protocol are not the strong suits of Americans, which is one reason why the Japanese tend to view us as large, loud water buffaloes, lumbering around without a clue, tromping and pooping all over their carefully arranged, exquisitely tended garden of a society. I certainly *felt* like a water buffalo when I got off the plane at Narita Airport, mumbling my one word of Japanese, taking my long vowels seriously, and weighing approximately four hundred pounds more than when I got on.

2

ADAPTING TO AN EXOTIC AND SOPHISTICATED CULTURE

Or: Bowing, Farting, etc.

I took an immediate liking to the Japanese culture, because it has a fascinating and wonderful quality that, for want of a better term, I will call "lack of height." I have read that, on the average, the Japanese are getting taller, but at the moment they seem to be about the same height as American junior-high-school students, only with fewer guns.

Throughout my adult life, I have described myself as being "about six feet tall," which is how American men describe themselves when they are about five-nine. Growing up, I was always one of the smaller, punier boys, the kind of boy who could be easily lifted up by other boys and held upside down over the toilet. I was also a late bloomer.[1] At parties in eighth grade, when the other kids were turning out the lights and necking, I was the dweeb who was putting the little plastic inserts into the 45 rpm records. So I was never a physically confident person. To this day I'm easily intimidated by large, physical men. I'll go to, say, an auto-tire store, needing to buy one new tire, and a man named Chuck, each of whose forearms is the size of Danny DeVito, will look at my car, then turn to me and, while poking his finger partway through my chest, say: "Whoa, pal, you don't need *one* new tire; you need *four* new tires. Don't he need four new tires, Bud?" And Bud, who's even larger than Chuck— who is, in fact, larger than some state capitols— will say: "Oh, he needs *at least* four. He might need six." Ultimately I'll wind up simply agreeing, in writing, to put all of their children through college.

But in Japan I was *big*. I started noticing as soon as we got off the plane. We were walking

---

[1] Or, in modern terminology, Puberty Impaired.

through a crowded airport concourse, and I realized that I could look over the top of everybody else's head.

"Hey!" I remarked to Beth. "I'm the tallest person in this concourse!"

This was a recurring observation of mine for the entire time we were in Japan. We'd be in some beautiful temple, or an important museum, and Beth and Robby would be having significant cultural experiences, and I'd be saying: "Hey! I'm the tallest person in this temple or museum!"

I wanted to buy a basketball and walk around Tokyo dribbling it, in case we happened to walk past a playground. The players, noting my height, would naturally ask me to play center, and I'd use my inside power game to muscle in many key points and block some crucial shots, and then later on, when my new friends and I were enjoying postgame beers and masculine camaraderie, I'd modestly reveal to them that in the United States, a lot of people called me Doctor Bad-Ass.[2]

Unfortunately, there didn't seem to be any playground basketball games in Tokyo, so I'd have looked pretty stupid dribbling a basketball around. Much of the time I managed to look stupid even without a basketball because, like most foreigners in Japan, I was constantly doing the wrong thing. Here you should prepare yourself for one of the

---

[2] Or, as the Japanese say, "Oh-GAH-tse-wah-na-KAH-no-mah-ska-wo."

searing insights that make this the book that it is[3] —*Japanese culture is different from ours*. For one thing, it consists almost entirely of Japanese people. For another thing, they don't shake hands.[4] They bow. They're not big on physical contact, especially with strangers. They'd be uncomfortable at a typical American social gathering, where people who barely know each other will often kiss and hug, and people who are *really* close will sometimes have sexual relations right in the foyer.

The Japanese are also formal about names, generally addressing each other with the honorary title "san," as in "Osaka-san," which is like saying "Mr. Osaka." I understand that, even if two Japanese have worked together for many years, neither would dream of using the other's first name. Whereas Americans are on a first-name basis immediately, and by the end of the first day have generally graduated to "Yo, Butthead!"

One night in Tokyo we watched two Japanese businessmen saying good-night to each other after what had clearly been a long night of drinking, a major participant sport in Japan. These men were totally snockered, having reached the stage of inebriation wherein every air molecule that struck caused them to wobble slightly, but they still managed to behave more formally than Americans do at funerals. They faced each other and bowed

---

[3] As opposed to *War and Peace*.

[4] I have no idea how they make personal wagers.

deeply, which caused both of them to momentarily lose their balance and start to pitch face-first to the sidewalk. Trying to recover their balance, they both stepped forward, almost banging heads. They managed to get themselves upright again and, with great dignity, weaved off in opposite directions. If both of them wound up barfing into the shrubbery, I bet they did it like Alfonse and Gaston, in a formal manner.

I never really did get accustomed to all the bowing. According to the guidebooks, there's an elaborate set of rules governing exactly how you bow, and who bows the lowest, and when, and for how long, and how many times, all of this depending on the situation and the statuses of the various bowers involved. Naturally, my family and I, being large, ignorant foreign water buffaloes, were not expected by the Japanese to know these rules. Nevertheless we did feel obligated to attempt to return bows when we got them.

This happened quite often. It started when we arrived at our hotel in Tokyo. As I was descending the steps of the airport bus, two uniformed bellmen came rushing up and bowed to me. Trying to look casual but feeling like an idiot, I bowed back. I probably did it wrong, because then *they* bowed back. So *I* bowed back. The three of us sort of bowed our way over to where the luggage was being unloaded, and I bowed to our suitcases, and the bellmen, bowing, picked them up and rushed into the hotel. We followed them past a bowing doorman into the hotel, where we were gang-bowed by hotel employees. No matter which direction we turned, they were aiming bows at us, sometimes from as far as twenty-five yards away.

Bobbing like drinking-bird toys, we bowed our way to the reception desk, where a bowing clerk checked us in. Then we bowed our way over to the elevators, where we encountered our first Elevator Ladies. These are young, uniformed, relentlessly smiling women who stand by the elevators in hotels and stores all day. Their function is to press the elevator button for you. Then, when the elevator comes, they show you where it is by gesturing enthusiastically toward it, similar to the way that models gesture on TV game shows when they are showing some lucky contestant the seventeen-piece dinette set that he has just won.

"Here is your elevator!" is the message of this gesture. "Isn't it a beauty?"

Throughout our stay in Japan, every Elevator Lady managed to give the impression that she was genuinely thrilled that I had chosen to ride her elevators, as opposed to some other form of vertical transportation. I never saw one who seemed to resent the fact that she was stuck in, let's face it, a real armpit of a job. If I did their work, it would turn me into a stark raving lunatic. Within days I'd be deliberately ushering people into open elevator shafts.

Anyway, we got into our hotel elevator, and the E.L. stood outside and bowed deeply as the doors closed. I bowed back, but not too low, for fear of getting my head caught in the doors. Alone in the elevator, I wondered if maybe all the bowing had been some kind of elaborate prank on us, and if at that very moment the hotel employees were all giving each other high-five handslaps and laughing so hard that they drooled on their uniforms.

We got to our room, and seconds later the bellmen knocked at the door, bowed their way inside, laid out our luggage, and checked to make sure that the room was OK. Then—this was an amazing event to witness—they *left*. They just *walked out of the room*.

An American bellman, of course, stands around in a congenial yet determined manner, waiting for you to figure out that you have not tipped him yet. If it doesn't dawn on you right away, he'll start telling you about some of the hotel's available special guest services, such as breakfast; or start demonstrating various deluxe features of the room, such as that it has electric lights, which you can operate via switches. If necessary he will stay in your room all night. You get up at 3:00 A.M. to go to the bathroom, and there is your bellman, showing you where the flush handle is and just generally continuing to be helpful until you spontaneously decide to give him a token of your gratitude.

But there's no tipping in Japan. You just don't do it. Even in restaurants. When people serve you

in some manner, you simply say "Thank you,"[5] DAVE BARRY DOES JAPAN
and they don't get angry or anything. In fact, they
often seem happy to have had the opportunity to
serve you, if you can imagine. This was quite a
shock for me, coming from a country where you
regularly find yourself tipping people just so they
won't spit on you.

The mysterious thing about all this is that
Japan—ask anybody who has been there—has superb service. And not just in nice hotels. Everywhere. You walk into any store, any restaurant, no
matter how low-rent it looks, and I bet you that
somebody will immediately call out to you in a
cheerful manner. This happened to us all over. I
never understood what the people were *saying,* of
course. They could have been saying: "Hah! Americans! We will eventually purchase your entire nation and use the Lincoln Memorial for tofu
storage!" But they always *sounded* friendly and
welcoming. And they were always eager to wait on
us. I couldn't help but think of the many times I've
been in American stores, especially large ones, attempting to give somebody some money in exchange for merchandise—which I always thought
was the whole *point* of stores—but was unable to
do so because the store employees were too busy
with other, higher-priority activities, such as talk-

---

[5] As follows: "Thank you."

ing or staring into space. More than once, in America's stores, I have felt like an intruder for trying to give money to clerks. "Oh great" is their unspoken but extremely clear attitude. "Here we had everything going nice and smooth, and along comes this *doofus* who wants—of all things!—to make a *purchase*. In a *store*, for God's sake."

I'll give you another example of what I'm talking about. We've traveled extensively in the United States, and often our son travels with us, and when he does we always try to arrange to have one of those folding beds for him in our hotel room. Beth always calls the hotel in advance and asks them to please write down that we want a folding bed. She calls later to confirm that there will be a folding bed. When we check in, we always remind them that we need a folding bed.

So needless to say, there has never—not *once*, in ten years, in dozens and dozens of hotels—been an actual folding bed in our room when we got there. We *always* have to call Housekeeping to ask for it, and nothing happens, so we call again, and maybe again, and of course Housekeeping is not happy about this—"*These damned guests! Always calling Housekeeping and requesting Housekeeping services!*"—and then finally, often late at night, our folding bed will be brought to us by a person who is obviously annoyed about having to deliver beds in the middle of the night to people who should have thought to arrange this earlier. Naturally, I always give this person a tip.

In Japan, the bed was always there, at every hotel, when we checked in. This may seem minor to you, but to us it was a miracle, comparable in scope to having a total stranger hold a door open for you in New York City.

I'll give you another minor but typical hotel example. When we checked into our hotel in Hiroshima, I noticed that our bathtub faucet would not produce hot water, so I called the front desk. In America, the front desk would have told me that somebody would be up to take a look at it, and eventually somebody would, but not necessarily during my current lifetime.

In Hiroshima, a bellman arrived at our room within, literally, one minute. He had obviously been sprinting, and he looked concerned. He checked the faucet, found that it was, indeed, malfunctioning, and—now looking *extremely* concerned—sprinted from the room. In no more than three minutes he was back with two more men, one of whom immediately went to work on the bathtub. The sole function of the other one, as far as we could tell, was to apologize to us on behalf of the hotel for having committed this monumentally embarrassing and totally unforgivable blunder.

"We are very sorry," he kept saying, looking as though near tears. "*Very* sorry."

"It's OK!" I kept saying. "Really!" But it did no good. The man was *grieving*.

The bathtub was fixed in under ten minutes, after which all three men apologized extravagantly

49

in various languages one last time, after which they left, after which I imagine that the hotel's Vice President for Faucet Operations was taken outside and shot.

No, just kidding. He probably took his own life. That's how seriously they take their jobs over there.

I keep reading that American businesses have figured out that they need to focus more attention on customer service, but I'm afraid we have a long way to go before we catch up to the Japanese. As I write these words, Beth and I are in a state of seething semihomicidal rage resulting from our repeated unsuccessful attempts to give money to Sears in exchange for fixing some problems with our refrigerator. Beth called the Sears Service Department two weeks ago and spoke to a Customer Service Representative who agreed to schedule a Repair Technician to come out. The Customer Service Representative was willing to tell Beth the *day* this would happen, but—you appliance-owners out there know how this works—she refused to reveal the *time* that the technician would be here.

This is because of National Security. If we knew the exact time that our appliance was being repaired, there is the danger that we might blurt this information out in public. We'd be in a restaurant, for example, and we'd have a few too many glasses of wine, and one of us would say, "Well, the Sears Refrigerator Repair Technician is coming to our house at two-thirty P.M. on Wednesday." We wouldn't even consider the possibility that the bus-boy lurking just a few feet away might be an enemy agent, and that we had blown the entire operation.

So when the day came, Beth stayed home all day, waiting for the Repair Technician, who of course did not show up. Probably Sears was just testing us, making sure that we really, sincerely wanted to have our refrigerator repaired and weren't just making service appointments for the sheer fun of it. So Beth spent the day on the phone with various Customer Service Representatives who were somewhat annoyed to be bothered about this problem, inasmuch as their job is to *schedule* service appointments, not to fritter away their time with irrelevant details such as whether or not the Repair Technician actually shows up.

The following morning, Beth—and I am afraid this is an example of the kind of "quitter" attitude that keeps so many Americans from achieving their full potential as measured by the percentage of working appliances in their homes—went to work. I was preparing to leave the house myself when I got a phone call from a man who identified himself as the Repair Technician. He re-vealed—despite the fact that we were talking on an unsecured phone line—that he was planning to take a look at our refrigerator *that very day.*

"What time?" I said, throwing caution to the winds.

"Before four o'clock," he said.

And so I stayed home all day, except for a

fifteen-minute span when I went to get my son at school, after leaving a message on the door that said: "SEARS—BE RIGHT BACK." My guess is that the Repair Technician, possibly disguised as a tree, was monitoring the house, and when I left the house, showing a flagrant lack of concern for his schedule, he moved on to the home of a more considerate appliance owner.

I don't mean to single out Sears here. Lots of companies, big and small, have a way of making you, the customer, feel that you rank, in the overall economic hierarchy, just below worm turds. Our house, being a house, is constantly trying to degenerate into a pile of random broken hardware, so we are constantly trying to get people to come fix things. We have learned to accept the fact that, even though these people have gone to the trouble and expense of *buying advertisements* in which they claim that they are in the business of fixing things, many of them will not show up. As homeowners, we've reached the point where we almost don't care whether the people really do anything, as long as they come to our house when they say they will. They could just show up, do nothing, and tell us we owe them $47.50, and we'll pay out of sheer gratitude.

I'll tell you what American businesses do a good job of: pretending to care about customers. I'm thinking particularly of TV commercials. Sears has *great* TV commercials, with relentlessly cheerful employees licking the shoes of satisfied custom-

ers. Likewise General Motors has Mr. Good-
wrench, who's always smiling and wearing a
freshly pressed uniform and returning a repaired
car to a delighted owner, against the backdrop of a
ludicrously hygienic garage filled with industrious
auto technicians who are clearly capable of repair-
ing the space shuttle. Has any U.S. automobile
owner, with any brand of car, ever actually encountered a repair department like this? Is it not fair to
say that most of the time, in real life, Mr. Good-
wrench is a guy who thinks maybe you can have
your car back by a week from next Halloween,
unless it turns out there's something *wrong* with it,
in which case he'll have to order parts from the
Distribution Center, which is located in Kurdistan?

And when you walk into McDonald's or
Burger King or Wendy's, are you typically greeted
by employees singing and dancing with ecstatic joy
over the opportunity to serve you? Or do you more
often find them to be downright sullen as a result of
the fact that they're stuck in jobs where not only do
they get paid the minimum wage, but they also
have to wear stupid hats?

Not that I'd be any better. I'd be sullen, too, if
I worked at McDonald's. I'd *much* rather be a
writer getting paid to complain about bad service.
And I'm sure that advertising people would much
rather have jobs wherein they make commercials
about fixing cars or serving hamburgers than jobs
where they'd actually have to *do* those things. And
every year approximately 17 million more Ameri-

cans decide that they'd rather become lawyers and spend their days wearing and filing suits, instead of doing some form of work that anybody actually needs. Too many chiefs, not enough Native Americans, that's what's wrong with this country. We all want to manage. We all want to attend meetings and develop concepts. We look down on jobs that involve any physical activity more rigorous than faxing. Nobody in this country knows how to *do* anything anymore. There was a time when average Americans could get together and, in one afternoon, build an entire barn. Yes! A barn! Can you imagine average Americans doing that today? Not a chance! They'd spend weeks debating the membership and organizational structure of the Barn Architect Selection Committee, whose members would then get into a lengthy squabble over the design of the logo to appear on their letterhead. Ultimately this issue would become a bitter and drawn-out dispute, be taken to court, and the people involved would start complaining of depression and anxiety, and psychologists would announce that these people were victims of a new disease called Barn Committee Logo Dispute Distress Syndrome, or BCLDDS, which would become the subject of one-hour shows by Phil Donahue and Sally Jessy Raphael, after which *millions* of Americans would realize that they, too, were suffering from BCLDDS, and they'd form support groups with Hot Line numbers and twelve-step programs.

That's what we modern Americans do. Anything

but actually BUILD THE DAMN BARN. Anything
but actually PICK UP A DAMN HAMMER AND
A DAMN PIECE OF LUMBER AND
SLAP!

Thanks, I needed that. Please excuse me for raving. The point I'm trying to make is that, in Japan,[6] people seem to be generally more diligent about doing their jobs, no matter how menial the jobs are. One afternoon in Tokyo we walked past a man who was down on his knees on the sidewalk *cleaning a public trash can.* He was wiping it briskly with a cloth and some blue chemical cleanser. Can you imagine anybody doing that job in the United States? Can you imagine that job even *existing?* No chance! I sure as hell wouldn't do that job. Neither would you. *Nobody* would. It would be beneath *everybody's* dignity. If a judge sentenced convicted child-murderers to do that job, they'd file lawsuits alleging cruel and unusual punishment. Environmental groups would claim that the cleaning chemical might harm the environment, and the government would require lengthy studies to determine whether trash-can cleaning posed a threat to several endangered species of fly, and of course these studies would have to be done by contractors who could prove that they hired the correct percentage of every known minority group including Norwegians, and

---

[6] Which is, in case you forgot, the topic of this book.

Sorry. It won't happen again. It's just that over the years there have been so many long, scholarly articles and books seeking to explain how come the Japanese have been kicking our economic butts all over the world, and the answer seems obvious as hell once you get over there: *They work harder.* They come to work earlier, they leave later, and a lot of them work on weekends. While we were in Japan, there was much public discussion of a government program intended to get Japanese workers to stop working so hard, if you can imagine. Apparently this has been a difficult program to implement. I bet the workers assigned to it are all putting in overtime.

I'm not saying this nose-to-the-grindstone approach is better. I think it has definitely held Japan back in some areas, such as music and humor,[7] and the ability to just hang loose with no purpose whatsoever, which many Americans can do effortlessly for decades at a time. What I'm about to say is extremely presumptuous, considering my abysmally limited knowledge of Japanese culture, but I'll say it anyway: I think Japan isn't as much *fun* as the United States. If countries were TV-show characters, Japan would be Sergeant Joe Friday on the old *Dragnet,* wearing a suit, filmed in black and white, grinding away at his job, getting just the

---

[7] More on music and humor later.

facts. America would be Norm on *Cheers:* He also has a job, but only so he can afford beer. Sergeant Friday is responsible and conscientious, the cement of society; Norm is the one you'd hang around with.[8]

Which is not to say that you shouldn't go there. You should. It's fascinating, and they have really clean taxis. But it's also a major adjustment for Americans, and not just because of the bowing. There's also the issue of nose blowing: According to the guidebooks, the Japanese think it's disgusting. They would no more blow their noses in public than . . . well, forget it. They are especially repelled by the idea of nose blowing in restaurants. (The result of this, of course, is that when you're in a Japanese restaurant, all you can think about is blowing your nose.) I imagine it must be a real treat for the Japanese when they visit the United States, where people, especially men, will routinely haul out large handkerchiefs in public, lean way back, and lunge violently forward while issuing window-shatteringly-loud, wet horselike snorts; then they critically examine their output, fold it up carefully, and stick it back into their pockets, as though dealing with rare gems.

The ironic thing is, the Japanese don't mind public displays of another bodily activity from which Americans tend to distance themselves. Beth

---

[8] You may feel that these are flagrant generalizations. Tough.

taught me this on our second night in Tokyo, as we were recounting the day's activities.

"I heard two farts today," she said.

"What?" I said. "I mean, where?"

"Out on the street, walking around,"[9] she said.

"Really?" I said.

"Really," she said. "You're allowed to fart in public here."

Beth claimed she saw this in a guidebook, although it might just have been a humorous attempt on her part to trick me into making a fool out of myself during a formal interview with an industry leader by standing up and letting go with a Force 10 pants-buster. So I remained my usual discreet self over there.

I needed to be unobtrusive while I quietly gathered information about stories of major international importance such as the eel shortage, which I'll get to in the next chapter.[10]

---

[9] Meaning *she* was walking around. Not the farts. Presumably.

[10] Unless I forget.

3

LOST IN TOKYO

Or: Looking for Plastic Squid

I'll get the bad news out of the way right up front, and discreetly: Tokyo is ugly. It looks as if it were hit by an anti-charm missile. It had the bad fortune of being almost entirely rebuilt after World War II, during what architectural historians refer to as the Age of Making Everything Look Like a Municipal Parking Garage, but Without the Warmth.

59

Also it is not what you would call a carefully planned city. You have your apartment buildings right next to your factories, which are right next to your restaurants, which are right next to your elevated roadways, which are right next to your parks, which are right next to your warehouses, which are right next to your monasteries, which are right next to your gambling parlors, which are right next to your office buildings, which are right next to your religious shrines, which are right next to your vending machines, which are right next to your cemeteries, which are right next to your bars, which are right next to your schools, which are right next to your dirty-comics stores,[1] which are right next to your nice department stores, which are right next to your hospitals, which are right next to your street vendors selling some kind of seafood delicacy that looks like sliced whale uvula. And that would be *one block*.

And this goes on for miles. Tokyo is huge. Something like 15 million people live there, and my estimate is that at any given moment, 14.7 million of them are lost. This is because the Tokyo street system holds the world outdoor record for randomness. A map of Tokyo looks like a tub of hyperactive bait. There is virtually no street that goes directly from anywhere to anywhere.

Adding to the excitement is the fact that *al-*

---

[1] OK, this one makes some sense.

most none of the streets have names. You think I'm kidding, right? Oh, you knew it? No matter. Look at a map of Tokyo. Look at a detailed map. Look for street names. There are hardly any. This is one of the biggest, busiest, most important cities in the world, and *most of the streets don't have names*. Ha-ha! That's a good joke on YOU, Mr. or Mrs. Visitor!

But wait! There's more. On these streets without names, there are buildings with meaningless numbers. Yes! Number 17 could be right next door to Number 341, which could be miles from Number 342 and 15.

So getting to an unfamiliar destination in Tokyo is basically a matter of going on the treasure hunt from hell, especially if you don't speak or read Japanese. You need to get extremely specific directions. "OK," the person directing you will say, "when you get to the subway stop, leave by exit 3A, next to the whiskey advertisement that shows a woman dancing with a robot, and turn *left* at the top of the stairs, going past a little shrine with a statue of Buddha that looks like Telly Savalas on cortisone, then you go down the street until you see a toy store with a display of girls' purses with a Felix the Cat motif, and right there is another little street, and you go left on that until you come to a man selling whale uvulas, then you turn. . . ."

And so on. One night Beth and I were with a group attempting to locate a bar we had heard about. All of these people lived in Tokyo, and one was Japanese, and this was a well-known bar, and we had the address, and we were right in the neighborhood. It took us about an hour to find it. We had to home in on it by making a series of telephone calls, like espionage agents setting up a clandestine meeting.

"Where are you now?" the bar people would say.

"We're at a green telephone next to a vending machine for Cabin Cigarettes," we would answer.

"You're getting closer," the bar people would say. "Call again when you see a yellow telephone next to a parked red bicycle." Etc.

Taxi rides in Tokyo were adventures in disorientation. God alone knows how the drivers knew where they were going. We'd be riding along a reasonable-sized street, then *yikes* the driver would swerve into a dark alley approximately the width of Peewee Herman, and then, after several blocks of missing pedestrians by molecules, we'd suddenly veer back onto another major street, but then *eeeek* we'd be back in an alley and *OH, NO* we're going into a *BUILDING* we're going up the *STAIRS* we're in somebody's *APARTMENT* pleasepleaseplease slow down *LOOK OUT FOR THE BATHTUB!*

I am exaggerating only slightly. But that's what it *felt* like. This is not to criticize the taxi drivers, who were courteous and highly professional. Many of them wear uniforms, sometimes including gloves, and they keep their cabs spotless.

Some of them put those little doily things on the seats. It was a stark contrast to the situation in, for example, New York, where, by law, before a taxi is assigned to the third-world sociopath who will be driving it, the rear seat must spend a minimum of six months in the intensive care unit of the body odor clinic.

We couldn't take many taxis in Tokyo, because we had no way to tell the drivers where we wanted to go. We often rode the subways, which are also (of course) clean and efficient, but sometimes very crowded. No doubt you've seen photos of Japanese subway workers shoving commuters into a subway car that's already visibly bulging. Of course subway workers would never try a crazy stunt like that in the United States. There would instantly be fifty-seven commuters writhing on the platform, screaming "Whiplash!" But the Japanese tend to be far more cooperative and docile and group-oriented. It would be easier to get the entire population of Tokyo to wear matching outfits than to get any two randomly selected Americans to agree on pizza toppings.

In fact, at times it seemed as though the entire population of Tokyo already *was* wearing matching outfits. All the men seemed to be wearing dark suits, white shirts, and dark ties. All the women seemed to be wearing darkish conservative dresses, often with hats and high heels. All the children seemed to be wearing some kind of school uniform. It was like a giant funeral. We didn't wear particularly casual clothes over there, but we always felt like the Three Hippie Tourists. Not that anybody ever said anything. Nobody ever hassled us about anything in Japan, where open confrontations about anything are considered horrendously embarrassing to everybody. But people always noticed us. Whenever I happened to glance up in the subway, I'd catch people staring at us, not in a hostile way, but frankly curious, because we were different, and I think the Japanese find being different fascinating, because it's the one thing, above all, that they're raised not to be.

I also noticed that, in crowd situations, they tended to give us a little more space. I'd heard that some Japanese think that foreigners, speaking of the body odor clinic, smell bad. I noticed maybe a half-dozen instances when people chose to stand rather than take an empty subway seat next to me. Twice, when I sat down, the person next to me got up, moved a few feet away, and stood. After a while I found myself routinely taking unobtrusive sniffs at my armpits. I considered learning how to make certain hygiene-related statements in Japanese, so that when I got on the subway, I could turn to Beth and say in a conversational tone of voice, "Well, we may be foreigners, but we certainly take showers every day!"

Of course I probably never could have learned a sentence of that magnitude, seeing as how I was having so much trouble remembering "thank you." The language barrier, combined with Tokyo's lunatic street system, meant that we spent a lot of time lost. I gave up asking for directions, because people never understood me, but they felt obligated to try to help anyway. It wasn't like in major U.S. cities, where if people don't know the directions, or just don't want to bother, they'll come right out and inform you, with that refreshing American directness, that your best bet is to go fuck yourself.

In Japan, I found that, by asking strangers for directions, I was placing this awful *burden* on them. The first time this happened, we were in a Tokyo station, trying to find the Japan Rail information bureau. I walked up to a briefcase-carrying businessman and said, hopefully, "Excuse me, do you speak English?" He did not, a fact that he indicated by looking extremely embarrassed and apologetic, conveying, via bodily language, the message: "What an *idiot* I am! Here I am, a Japanese person, in Japan, and I can't even speak *English!* I should pull a sword out of this briefcase and disembowel myself right here in the station!"

I attempted to communicate my problem by saying "Information?" while pointing to my Japan Rail brochure and shrugging elaborately with a facial expression of great puzzlement bordering on imbecility. He adopted an expression of intense interest, took the brochure, and said "in-fo-ma-shan." He said this a couple of times, frowning at the brochure. Then he looked up and frowned at the station for a while.

"In-fo-ma-shan," he said again. He clearly

had no clue what this meant, but I had asked him for help, and he was not about to be so horrendously impolite as to abandon me.

"In-fo-ma-shan," he said. Then he walked a few steps, possibly to indicate that progress was being made, and he frowned at the brochure again.

"In-fo-ma-shan," he said.

I began to realize that this man would probably spend the day there with me, maybe several days, maybe lose his job, rather than walk away from his obligation. So I gently took the brochure away from him and said, "Thank you! Thank you!" while walking backward and holding my hands out to indicate that he did not have to follow. He was hugely relieved. He began bowing violently toward me, smiling, overcome with gratitude, clearly thinking, *What a kind and generous foreigner! Allowing me to keep my job! And he didn't smell that bad!*

This was typical of our experiences. The Japanese weren't particularly eager to get involved with us, because it was so hard to communicate, but when they *did* get involved, they were relentlessly conscientious. So we found that it was easier to just remain lost most of the time.

We never found half the things we were looking for. For example, we spent a large chunk of one afternoon in Tokyo going around the same block approximately 157 times, looking for a store that sold nightingale poop. Really. Beth had a guide-book, which unfortunately I can't seem to find now, that said that this certain neighborhood had this little store that sold some rare cosmetic product made from . . . nightingale poop. As a cultural explorer, I thought this was fascinating,[2] so we tried to find the store, but naturally the Japanese character for nightingale poop would not be something so logical as this:

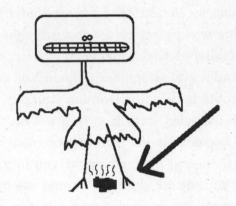

So we never did find it. We did, however, locate the Plastic Food District. This was actually pretty easy. I would imagine that Tokyo has the largest plastic-food industry in the world. This is because many Japanese restaurants advertise their menu items by means of window displays featuring plastic models of the various entrees, desserts, and beverages. Many of these models are extremely detailed and lifelike, which can be scary to a Westerner, because the Japanese routinely eat things

---

[2] In the sense of "really stupid."

that have eyeballs or suckers or other flagrantly unacceptable organs still attached to them. No effort is made to hide this. In fact, it seems to be a *selling* point. So you'd pass by a restaurant window, and you'd see a plastic model of what would otherwise be an OK-looking dish, but lunging menacingly out of the noodles will be a tentacle, similar to the one on the giant squid that attacked the submarine in *20,000 Leagues Under the Sea.* (You almost expected to see it clutching a detailed plastic model of Kirk Douglas.)

Squid is quite popular in Japan. You can order it as a topping on your Domino's pizza.[3] Another popular tentacled item is octopus. You see food stands decorated with cartoons of Mister Happy Octopus, waving his tentacles at you in a friendly manner to indicate that you should eat him. You can eat your octopus on a stick, or you can have fried octopus balls.[4]

But the big item when we were there was eels. It was eel season. Everywhere we went, there were window displays of eels, sometimes alive. Also there were sidewalk vendors openly grilling eels on sticks. This was appalling to me, because it is evident to any objective party that eels are nothing more than large slime-covered seagoing worms. The only Western person I know who has ever

---

[3] Of *course* they have Domino's Pizza in Japan.

[4] The male octopus has eight. (Rim shot.)

voluntarily eaten eels is my former newspaper editor, Gene Weingarten, who also chews rubber bands for relaxation and once knowingly ate a piece of dog. But the Japanese were snorking down eels like there was no tomorrow, to the point where they had an eel shortage, according to the newscaster on the English-language cable channel in our hotel. She said the Japanese eat 100,000 tons of eel per year. To give you an idea of how much that is, if you were to place 100,000 tons of eels end to end, starting in San Francisco, your hands would be disgusting.

As bold culinary adventurers, we experimented with all kinds of Japanese food for about fifteen minutes, then spent the rest of our trip looking for Kentucky Fried Chicken. Of course, sometimes we had to order Japanese food, in which case we would order the most Western-looking thing on the menu, such as spaghetti. But you never knew what you'd find in there. Corn kernels, for example, popped up everywhere, including in the spaghetti sauce, fried eggs, and one item I ate that was supposed to be a hamburger. One restaurant we walked past had, as its window display, a giant plastic ear of corn, maybe six feet long. That was the entire display. I gather that the Japanese are quite fond of corn. I gather that sometimes the men come home from work and say to their spouses: "I feel like corn tonight! Let's go to the Giant Ear of Corn Restaurant."

In a small resort town called Beppu, we walked past a restaurant with a sign, in English, proclaiming that this was "The Loving Singing Eating Italian Tomato Restaurant." The centerpiece of the plastic-food display was a plate of plastic spaghetti with a large, very lifelike crab claw lunging up out of it, as if waving. "Help!" Mr. Crab is saying. "I am trapped in a plate of spaghetti!"

Our general policy at restaurants, if there was nothing Western-looking available, was to order whatever dish had been most thoroughly processed and cooked and otherwise altered from its natural eyeball-intensive state. Even then we could never be sure. One evening in Kyoto we ate at a restaurant where you ate various things on a stick. You sat at a counter, and three cooks bustled around preparing things, and every three or four minutes they'd place a stick with something on the end of it in front of each customer. (When you were done eating, you paid an amount based on the number of empty sticks you had.)

The three cooks spoke a little English, so when they placed a new set of sticks in front of us, they'd announce what it was. "CRAB!" they'd say. Or: "POTATO!" We were enjoying this, because it was interesting and the food tasted good, and so when they came around with maybe the tenth set of sticks, I unhesitatingly took a big bite. I was chewing away at some crunchy substance when the three cooks, looking very pleased with themselves, announced: "CRICKET!"

"Gack," I said, spitting it out but being careful not to look directly at it.

"You can have mine," said my son, who ate virtually nothing for the remainder of the trip except white rice and pretzels.

Japanese chefs at certain kinds of restaurants yell a lot. They'll yell a greeting when customers enter, and thank-yous when they leave. I always yelled "thank you" back, because they generally had knives. We went to one restaurant that featured a style of cuisine called *robatayaki,* wherein the customers sit around a huge table covered with food—all kinds of fresh vegetables, meat, fish with their heads still on, large scary crabs that look as though they might spring to their feet and stride over and pinch your nose, and so on. In the middle of the table, surrounded by the food, are two chefs wearing samurai-style headbands and kneeling in front of very hot cooking devices. When the chefs get your order, they instantly grab whatever ingredient they need, attack it with large sharp knives, cook it super-hot, then hand it directly to you on a long-handled wooden paddle while shouting something.

Constantly circling the table are several waiters, taking new orders (you order a lot of different dishes in *robatayaki*) and shouting them out to the cooks, who shout back, which sometimes causes other waiters to shout things. So basically the staff is shouting all the time about everything the customers are eating. I mean everything. I'd order another beer,[5] and the waiter would shout something that I was told was Japanese for "ASAHI [a brand of beer] SUPER DRY BEER!" He'd sprint off to get it while another waiter and both cooks, just keeping everybody informed, would also shout "ASAHI SUPER DRY BEER!" This also happened when I asked for *water*. I wasn't about to ask where the men's room was. ("HE'S GOING TO TAKE A LEAK!")

I certainly would never say anything judgmental about another culture, but in certain food-related areas, the Japanese are clinically insane. The new culinary rage when we were in Japan was to eat fish *that were still alive*. I cannot imagine doing such a thing unless I were really desperate to get into a fraternity, but according to news reports, people were paying top yen in fine Tokyo restaurants for live, gasping fish. The waiter brings you your fish, still gasping,[6] then quickly slices it open right at your table; then you're supposed to eat it while the fish is staring at you with its nearer eyeball and a facial expression that says, "Go ahead and enjoy yourself! Don't mind me! I'll be dead fairly soon!"

And that's not the weirdest culinary activity that the Japanese engage in. There is also *fugu*. This is a kind of blowfish that the Japanese eat raw. So far, you are not surprised. You are saying: "Big

---

[5] Beer is a recurring literary theme in this book.

[6] I mean the fish is gasping, although I suppose the waiter could be, too.

deal, the Japanese eat a lot of fish raw." Well, what you are apparently not aware of, Mr. or Ms. Smarty Pants, is that *fugu* contains a *lethal poison.* The liver of the male and the ovaries of the female contain one of the most toxic substances in nature, for which there is no antidote, which means that if your *fugu* is not prepared *exactly right,* with *all* of the dangerous organs removed, you have encountered the Blowfish of Doom and soon are going to meet the Big Maitre d' in the Sky.

Clearly this is a fish that Mother Nature is telling us we should leave the hell under water, but to the Japanese it is a great delicacy. Every year they eat tons of it. They'll pay the equivalent of hundreds of dollars to eat it. And every year several people die because their *fugu* was prepared wrong.

I suppose it probably wouldn't be so scary if you ate *fugu* prepared by a trained professional chef,[7] but suppose you were invited to dinner in somebody's home, and the host decided to pull out all the stops and really give you a treat?

HOSTESS: Guess what?
YOU: What?
HOSTESS: Roger's making *fugu*!
YOU: *WHAT?*
ROGER *(who has clearly had a few drinks, shouting from the kitchen):*
Yes! I picked this up today at a little place right next to the whale-uvula stand! *(He*

---

[7] Notice I say "you." *I'd* never do it.

waves a blowfish, which is a hideous greenish-black color and is puffed up with rage.) I'm going to prepare it now!

YOU *(hastily):* I hate to see you go to all that trouble. Maybe we should just . . .

ROGER *(starting to whack the blowfish apart with a knife):* Nonsense! This'll only take a second!

HOSTESS: Roger loves to cook.

ROGER *(holding up a fish part):* Honey, does this look like an ovary?

One useful Japanese phrase they should include in the guidebooks: "Does this particular dish kill you if prepared improperly?" Of course, at many Japanese restaurants, once you see your bill, you might wish you *had* consumed an improperly prepared blowfish, because the prices, especially in Tokyo, are extremely high. I cannot overemphasize the importance, if you go there, of having Random House pay for everything. And even then, you're going to want to draw the line on some expenditures. For example, I decided not to purchase a gift melon. Melons are prized by the Japanese, and at some of the nicer department stores, we found gift melons selling for upwards of $75 apiece. These were nice-looking melons, in nice little wood boxes, but still, $75 for a melon?

People told us that the Japanese are very big on giving gifts, and the idea with the melon is, the recipient will appreciate it, because he or she knows how much it cost. However, when you give a gift in

Japan, etiquette requires you to disparage it. "This melon is nothing," you might say. Or: "What a pathetic excuse for a melon I am giving you!" This is of course exactly the opposite of how we Americans would handle the giving of a $75 melon. If we gave somebody such a melon, the instant he unwrapped it, we'd be prodding him with our forefinger and saying, "Do you have any idea how much that melon *cost*?" We'd never be able to forget it. "Hi!" we'd say, introducing ourselves to people at parties years later. "My name is Bob. I once gave somebody a seventy-five-dollar melon!"

IDEA FOR GETTING RICH: Using genetic engineering, combine a melon with a black widow spider to produce a new kind of melon that will kill you instantly unless it is prepared exactly right. This would be a HUGE seller in Japan.

We did spend some money on plastic food, which we found in the Plastic Food District, which as you may recall is the topic I was attempting to raise several thousand words ago. I can't remember the Japanese name for this area, and I have no idea how we got there, so you'll just have to ask somebody.[8] It's well worth a visit. There are quite a few stores there with large displays of plastic food, in-

---

[8] It's not too far from the store that sells nightingale poop, if that's any help.

cluding some major tentacles. I was admiring one of these when I realized that Beth was actually *buying* some plastic food.

"Why are you buying plastic food?" I asked her calmly. She replied, and I want to stress that this is an actual quote: "Because they have such a terrific selection."

Of course, plastic food is only one of the attractions of Tokyo. There is also the famous Ginza district, which has very upscale department stores featuring gift melons as well as scarily expensive designer clothes, watches, jewelry, and other luxury items that the Japanese buy like crazy. A big reason why the Japanese spend so freely on luxuries, I was told, is that most of them see no point in trying to save for a house, because real estate in and around Tokyo is absurdly expensive. Most families live in apartments wherein the total living space is about the same as the area that the average American family uses to store the Cuisinart accessories. So it's not all luxury over there. They're living like chick-peas in a can and they have to wear funereal clothes and get stuffed into trains by transit workers and disparage their gift melons and eat grilled seagoing worms.

But there are also some really positive aspects to Japanese urban life, with some major ones being:

1. a very low crime rate
2. culture
3. beer in vending machines.

We'll have more on these topics in our next chapter, wherein we explore Tokyo night life and analyze Japanese society via the device of recalling the time in 1964 when Lanny Watts and I barfed on the chief of police's lawn. You won't want to miss it.

CHAPTER

4

THE TRADITIONAL JAPANESE ARTS

*Or: How I Married
a Grandmother*

After several days in Tokyo we decided to acquire an in-depth understanding of the traditional Japanese arts by taking the Hato Tour-Bus Company's Tokyo Nightlife Tour. We weren't at all nervous about touring Tokyo by night. This was partly because we knew we'd be surrounded by a dense protective clot of fellow tourists, but mainly because Japan has a low crime rate, unless you count the fact that approximately every fifteen minutes the entire Cabinet gets indicted for taking bribes.

So they do have high-level scandals, but there's little street crime. You'd be amazed at what passes for crime in Japan. One day in Tokyo I picked up an English-language newspaper called the *Asahi Evening News,* which had a large photograph and a story about—prepare to be shocked— *lamppost graffiti*. Yes. Somebody was going around the city of Nagoya writing "Sagi Nomura" on lampposts. "Sagi" means "swindler." The graffiti writer was commenting on Japan's scandal *du jour,* which was the giant Nomura securities firm's admission that it had been compensating its large clients—but not small investors—for their stock losses. The newspaper story said:

"Such graffiti reproaching securities houses has been drawn on at least 29 lampposts and traffic signal poles in the business area of the city. All the markings are in chalk of several colors, including white, red, and yellow, and are believed to have been written by one person."

So there you have a Japanese-style crime wave. Terror Stalks the City. A mystery fiend was out there somewhere, prowling the streets, armed with *several colors of chalk.* For some reason this story was not reported in the United States, possibly because at that time the news media here were too busy updating the public on the number of heads found in Jeffrey Dahmer's refrigerator.

They follow the rules in Japan. More than once in Tokyo, late at night, I saw lone pedestrians standing on corners, with no traffic in sight, waiting patiently for the light to change so they could cross the street legally. In every city we saw bicycles left unattended everywhere, unlocked. People there just don't think about theft. In Kyoto we spent a couple of days with a wonderful guide named Kunio Kadowaki, who hardly ever locked his van, despite the fact that it was equipped with a TV, a VCR, a phone, and other expensive electronic gadgetry. I told him that in American cities, it's common for people to remove their radios when they leave their cars.

"Ha! Ha!"[1] he said. "That's very funny!"

Kunio said the reason people don't steal in Japan is basically that the social and economic penalties for any kind of nonconforming behavior are extremely high.

"In Japan you have one race, one time zone," he said. "Everybody is expected to act the same. Everybody must fit in. There are no wild cards here."

I asked him how Americans compared to Japanese.

He laughed. "All Americans are wild cards," he said.

---

[1] Kunio is the only person I've ever met who, when he laughs, actually says "Ha! Ha!" Just like it says in books.

In Japan, he said, you're simply not allowed to screw up. If a Japanese boy stole a bicycle, the parents would be horrified and ashamed beyond Western comprehension; they'd rush over to the victim's house, bearing gifts and apologizing profusely, because if the victim decided to press charges, the boy would never be able get into good schools, and therefore would never get a good job. His future would be trashed because of a bicycle.

"In Japan, if you have one bad spot in your life, it's very difficult to get it back," Kunio said. "If it's reported in the newspaper, the boy's life is almost over."

I'm glad we're not that strict in the United States, because my life would have been over a number of times before I got out of high school. I'm thinking particularly of a fall evening in Armonk, New York, in 1964, when Carmine Labriola, whose parents were out of town,[2] invited every young person on the immediate North American continent to his house for an elegant and sophisticated party (theme: "Let's Puke on Our Own Shoes"). My friend Lanny Watts and I attended this party, then attempted, using our six functioning brain cells as navigational aids, to walk back to my house. Here is a simplified map of the layout of Armonk at the time:

---

[2] And I hope, for their sake, that they never came home.

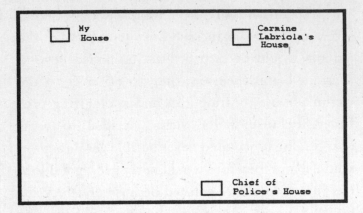

So it goes without saying that Lanny and I elected to take the following route:

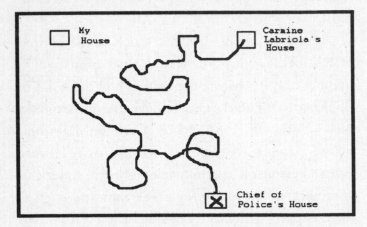

That's correct: Of all the homes in Armonk, New York, we managed to navigate to the one belonging to Chief of Police John Hergenhan, where we wisely decided to lie down on the lawn, throw up, and go to sleep, which is what we were doing when the chief, using the advanced criminology technique of looking out his window, detected us.

This performance got us into the newspaper. We were identified only as "drunken youths," but everybody knew who we were. We were famous.

"Let me get this straight," people would say. "You walked two miles so you could pass out on *the chief of police's lawn?*"

My parents were not at all happy about this, but I didn't get into any major long-term trouble. It was just one of a number of boyhood scrapes[3] that I got into as a result of being young and stupid, none of which prevented me from going on to college and a successful career in the competitive, demanding, and prestigious field of making booger jokes. Whereas in Japan, most of my friends and I, and probably you and *your* friends, would have been considered criminal wild-card outcasts from society.

So the Japanese tend to toe the line. But not necessarily because they want to; they have to. As Kunio Kadowaki told me: "Japan is a no-choice society." This is essentially the point of a fascinating and disturbing book called *The Enigma of Japanese Power,* by Dutch journalist Karel van Wolferen, which I strongly recommend if you're interested in reading a book about Japan by somebody who actually knows what he's talking about.[4] Van Wolferen argues that the standard Western

---

[3] Such as the incident with the traffic flares inside the diner, and I want to stress that all charges were dropped.

[4] As opposed to this book, for example.

view of the Japanese—that they naturally tend to be docile and group-oriented because they're so racially and culturally similar, and therefore lack individuality—is crap. He writes:

> I believe that the Japanese are individuals, all 120 million of them. Not all may want to assert their individuality; most, having been so conditioned, do not. But I have met quite a few who want to be taken for distinct persons, rather than as indistinct members of a group. These independent thinkers are disturbed. In many cases they have withdrawn into the private world of their own mind. Japanese culture harbors a vast, unconnected and uncharted archipelago of such private worlds. Individualistic Japanese are generally non-political because they would constantly burn their fingers if they were to challenge the existing power arrangements.

Despite its alleged transformation to a modern society, van Wolferen argues, Japan remains a highly oppressive place, where democratic central government is mainly a facade, and real power is exercised, as it has been for centuries, by what he calls "the System"—a complex arrangement of semiautonomous, nonelected groups, each of which rigidly controls some aspect of Japanese life. Those in power argue that the System simply reflects the Japanese people's cultural preference for conformity; but nobody ever asks the people. They're expected to shut up and go along, and nonconformists are penalized harshly. Every now and then somebody in the System gets really greedy or dumb, and there's a high-level scandal, and everybody acts upset, and some cosmetic reforms are implemented. But the System endures.

"Today," van Wolferen writes, "the most powerful groups include certain ministry officials, some political cliques and clusters of bureaucrat-businessmen. There are many lesser ones, such as the agricultural cooperatives, the police, the press and the gangsters."

Oh, yes—that's right: They have gangsters in Japan. The gangs are called yakuza, and their role in the System is to operate the extortion, loan-sharking, and prostitution industries. As long as they don't carry guns, sell drugs, or harm innocent civilians, the police pretty much leave them alone. The yakuza are about as clandestine as the National Football League. Everybody knows who they are. Many of them get large tattoos and chop off finger joints to demonstrate loyalty or some other important gangster quality. Also they're the only people in Japan who wear double-breasted suits, white ties, and sunglasses.

"Hi!" their outfits shout. "We're gangsters!"

Van Wolferen says the yakuza "openly maintain offices—adorned with gang emblems—in major cities." One gang even publishes an in-house magazine, which gives information about members in jail and helpful tips on how to be a better overall gangster.

The yakuza are one of only two groups in Japan who buy large American cars (the other group, don't ask me why, is dentists). I think that, if we're going to overcome our trade deficit with Japan, American car dealers should target this market more aggressively via advertising campaigns such as:

> CADILLAC. . . .
> "For the Discriminating Man Who Has Lopped Off the Ends of His Pinkies"

But my point is that even crime is carried on in an orderly fashion in Japan, and ordinary civilians have little reason to fear violence. Their lives are constricted, but their streets are safe. Old ladies ride the Tokyo subways alone at night, making no effort to protect their purses or shopping bags. Imagine if they tried an insane stunt like that in New York City. They'd be mugged in nanoseconds. There would be a brief flurry of activity, ignored by the other passengers—all of whom would be studying the subway advertisements for genital wart cures, secure in the knowledge that *their* belongings are attached to their bodies by steel cables bolted directly to the skeletal system—

and then the muggers would be gone, and the old

ladies would be sitting there stark naked. They'd probably be blamed for getting mugged, because they made it so easy. They might end up getting arrested on some charge like indecent exposure, or Being Really Naive on a Subway.

But in Japan they're safe, and we felt safe, except for the night our son dreamed that Godzilla was attacking Tokyo and we had to get up at 2:30 A.M. and peek out through the hotel curtains to make sure that the city was still intact. Other than that we never had a moment's nervousness about our physical safety when we were in Japan. Thus we did not hesitate to take the Hato Tour-Bus Company's Tokyo Nightlife Tour.[5]

Joining us on the bus were about two dozen other Westerners. As we drove through Tokyo, our guide, Mr. Sato, got on the public-address microphone and warmed us up for our big evening with a little stand-up comedy.

"Our driver is very good," he said. "No bad drivers in Tokyo. All bad drivers are dead." *(Pause for laughter.)*

After stopping for dinner, we went to our first Nightlife cultural stop, the famous Kabukiza Theater, where we watched a Kabuki play. Or part of a Kabuki play. I have here a guidebook clearly stating that Kabuki is the "height of artistic perfection" and an "unforgettable experience," so I have

---

[5] You anal compulsives can relax now. We're back to the actual topic of this chapter.

to conclude that the problem, on this particular evening, was me.

I should note first that I've never been a big fan of any kind of classical performing art form. I am severely bored by opera, for example. The only ballet I ever enjoyed was one I saw on an outdoor stage, where instead of a curtain they had a large hedge that the dancers could duck behind. In the climactic scene, the lead ballerina got picked up by one of the male dancers, who was apparently supposed to waft her effortlessly offstage, but he had trouble keeping her aloft, plus her tutu blocked his vision, so he lunged forward, building up a head of steam, and rammed her headfirst smack into the hedge. Then he backed up, changed course slightly and ran her into the hedge *again,* before he finally managed to stagger offstage, with shrubbery clinging to both of their costumes. I was moved to *tears.*

So when it comes to the classical arts, I'm basically an unsophisticated low-rent Neanderthal philistine kind of guy, which is why I'm probably just revealing my own intellectual limitations and cultural myopia when I tell you that Kabuki is the silliest thing I have ever seen onstage, and I have seen a man juggle two rubber chickens *and* a birthday cake.

For one thing, all the actors were wearing costumes that made them look like John Belushi on *Saturday Night Live* playing the part of the samurai delicatessen clerk, only with funnier haircuts. For another thing, since all Kabuki actors are male, a man was playing the role of the heroine. According to the program notes, he was a famous Kabuki actor who was extremely skilled at portraying the feminine character by using subtle gestures and vocal nuances perfected over generations. What he looked like, to the untutored Western eye, was a man with a four-year supply of white makeup,[6] mincing around the stage and whining. It was Belushi playing the samurai whining transvestite.

In fact, everybody seemed to whine a lot. It was all that happened for minutes on end. Kabuki has the same dramatic pacing as bridge construction. It's not at all unusual for a play to last *ten hours*. And bear in mind that one hour of watching Kabuki is the equivalent of seventeen hours spent in a more enjoyable activity, such as eye surgery.

From time to time, a member of the audience would yell something. This is also part of the Kabuki tradition; at key moments, audience members, sometimes paid by the performers, yell out a performer's family name, or words of appreciation.[7] Our guide, Mr. Sato, had cautioned us that this yelling had to be done in a certain traditional way, and that we should not attempt it. It was a

---

[6] Possibly made with nightingale poop.
[7] For example, according to one of the guidebooks, an audience member might yell, "I was looking forward to that!" Really.

good warning—although I'm not sure what I would have yelled anyway. Maybe something like: "NICE HAIRCUT!" Or: "WAY TO MINCE!"

But the silliest part was the plot. We were able to follow it by means of earphones attached to little rented radio sets, tuned to a broadcast interpretation of what the actors were whining about. We watched for an hour, and here, according to my notes, is:

The Plot

Everybody is upset and whining. One reason is that they lost the sacred incense burner. Another reason is that some little boy is blind. And the heroine is *extremely* upset because she has to sell herself to the brothel so that she can afford to purchase the ointment her boyfriend needs for his hip ailment.[8]

Meanwhile some assassins are lurking around.

So at this point, as you might expect, everybody stops for a few minutes to remember the way birds sing when they're alone.

Now the boy appears onstage. "He is blind," the interpreter informs us, "and earns money as a masseur."

The boy, played by a boy who was apparently selected for his ability to whine for extended

---

[8] I swear I am not making this plot up.

lengths of time in a extraordinary high pitch,
asks—why not?—whether his clogs are anywhere
around. Everybody whines about this for three
solid minutes (or fifty-one minutes in E.S.T., eye
surgery time).

At this point the heroine goes off to sell herself
to the brothel, which apparently has a big demand
for women who look like John Belushi. Then the
assassins reappear and the characters stage the
World's Least Realistic Sword Fight.

Then the assassins go away and the heroine
comes back and everybody squats around to
whine for a while. A man who has been doing
most of the whining—I think he might be the one
who lost the sacred incense burner—announces
suddenly (by which I mean, in only about five
minutes) that he is going to commit suicide. He
stabs himself in the gut, thereby causing a stirring
of hope to ripple through the audience as it appears that the play might possibly be coming to
an end.

But no. If you think this man could whine
before, you should see him when he has stabbed
himself. He kneels at center stage, holding his gut,
and squalls at the audience for fifteen minutes.
Meanwhile, other people appear and comment at
length on how tragic the situation is. It is. And
nobody *does* anything about it, such as call the
samurai paramedic unit. They just whine about it,
with the victim himself making more noise than
anybody.

"SOMEBODY STAB HIM AGAIN!" is what
I would have yelled, if I knew how in Japanese.

Finally he dies, possibly from overacting, and
another guy announces that he's going to go off and
find the sacred incense burner, and everybody is
happy, especially us culturally myopic tourists,
sprinting from the theater into the safety of the
Tokyo night.

Then we all got back onto the bus and went to
a geisha house, where Mr. Sato told us that we
were going to witness an authentic geisha ceremony, performed by authentic schooled geishas.
He said it was a dying art form, because young
women today no longer want to go into the geisha
field, which I can certainly understand, because
before you can become a geisha, you have to spend
years learning how to sing traditional songs and
arrange flowers in a traditional way and pour tea in
a ceremony so ancient and traditional and all-
around slow that it makes Kabuki theater seem like
a Madonna concert. It's not one of your modern,
fast-paced, high-octane professions. You seldom
see geishas wearing beepers and rushing off to perform emergency tea pourings.

In fact, you don't see young geisha girls at all,
because they're a dying breed. The geishas at the
house that we went to all seemed to be grandmoth-
ers at the very minimum. Also there were no Japanese customers there. I think this particular geisha
house has been catering in a traditional manner to
tour buses for thousands of years.

But the ladies were very nice. They told us to take off our shoes and sit at some low tables, and we all suffered from leg cramps while they served us beverages. I ordered a beer, which they served via the ancient traditional method of opening a bottle and putting it in front of me.

Next they performed some dances and songs for us, and then they announced that they were going to have a geisha courtship ceremony. They asked for an audience volunteer to serve as the suitor, and I stuck my hand up. Japanese beer will do that to you.

They brought me up onstage, put a kimono around me, and had me kneel on a pillow. Then they brought out the object of my affections, played by the head geisha, who was wearing a kimono and the traditional geisha facial cosmetics, which are apparently applied with a trowel. It looked like she had a half-inch-thick layer of plaster on her face. I'm sure she was a lovely person, but the overall effect was scary.

She danced around me, taking tiny steps and stopping every now and then to look sideways at me in what I assume was supposed to be a coquett-ish and flirtatious manner.

"Hey, Big Boy!" seemed to be the message of this dance. "You like my floral arrangements?"

Next she filled a ceremonial pipe with to-bacco, lit it, and handed it to me. I took a puff, emitted a ceremonial cough, and she took the pipe back. The narrator announced that this was the crucial part of the ceremony, because if she also puffed on the pipe, it meant that she had agreed to marry me. After a moment of extreme suspense, she took a puff, and everybody clapped and the two of us lovebirds went off arm in arm, presumably to our love nest, where, unable to control our passion any longer, we would chisel layers off her face and look at photos of her grandchildren.

That was the end of our Tokyo Nightlife Tour, although of course there is more to traditional Japanese culture than just Kabuki theater and geisha houses. There are many other classical disciplines, including haiku poetry and the important dramatic art forms Noh and Bunraku, which are discussed in detail in other chapters.[9] Also we will address modern Japanese culture, particularly the question of whether the Japanese are any good at rock 'n' roll.[10] But first we need to discuss Japanese industry, and how come they can make such good cars. By cheating, probably, in the ancient, traditional manner.

---

[9] Not in *this* book, however.
[10] No.

SECRETS OF
JAPANESE INDUSTRY

*I Probably
Should Have Written
Them Down*

You probably figured this out already, but
I'm not a real journalist. Oh, I work for the
Miami Herald, and I have a press card, and
I sometimes hang around with real reporters at
news events such as political conventions. But journalists produce accurate, responsible stories about
issues such as the energy policies of Paul E. Tson-

gas, whereas I produce stories about how you can rearrange the letters in "Paul E. Tsongas" to spell "Gaseous Plant."[1]

In Japan, however, I ran into the problem of being taken seriously. I kept trying to let people know that I was a humor writer. "I'm a humor writer," I would say, and then, by way of explanation, I would wink broadly and elbow them in the ribs and go: "Har!"

But the Japanese are very sensitive about the kind of press they get over here, so they tend to take *any* U.S. writer seriously. This is why I found myself, against my will, interviewing the president of the Federation of Economic Organizations (F.O.E.O., I suppose).

This interview was arranged for me by Hiroshi Ishikawa, who works for Japan's Foreign Press Center, and who helped me a lot, not only in setting up my itinerary, but also in just being a nice guy who speaks English well and could explain Japanese customs and procedures to my wife and me when we were bumbling around being big, stupid tourist water buffalo. For example, the day we met him, which happened to be a very hot, very bright summer day, I asked him why it was that, as far I could tell, my wife, my son, and I were the only three people in Japan wearing sunglasses. Hiroshi hemmed and hawed a little, clearly not comfortable

---

[1] Also "Get Nasal Soup." You can look this up.

with having to break the news, but eventually he explained that in Japan, people tend to associate sunglasses with gangsters. I never would have figured that out on my own, despite the fact that it appeared in a previous chapter. It was a good thing to know, although I continued to wear sunglasses anyway because I figured that if I had to be a water buffalo, at least I could be a vaguely *menacing* water buffalo.

I gave Hiroshi a couple of books I'd written, so he'd know what kind of writer I was, and I believe that he read them, because one night, after we had both had a couple of beers, he asked me a question that showed penetrating insight into not only my writing style, but also my attitude, my philosophy, and—yes—the moral values at the very core of my intellectual being.

"What is a 'booger'?" he said.

"Well," I said. "Umm."

"Yes?" he said.

"OK," I said. "You know your nose?"

"Yes," he said.

"OK," I said. "You know how sometimes, you, umm, you . . ."

"Yes?" he said.

". . . you sometimes get, you know, those things that you sometimes get?" I said. "In your nose?"

"Yes," he said.

"Those are boogers," I said.

"I see," he said, looking thoughtful and seeming to be not at all inclined to fall on the floor and roll around clutching his sides in an uncontrollable paroxysm of laughter. Sometimes these sophisticated humor concepts do not translate well into foreign cultures.

Anyway, Hiroshi understood that I was a humor writer. But as a representative of the Foreign Press Center, he seemed to feel obligated to help me acquire Significant Japan Facts. He was constantly giving me official information booklets, including *Education in Japan, Leisure and Recreational Activities, Japanese Women Yesterday and Today, Facts and Figures of Japan 1991,* and *The Current State of Japanese Industry.* Unfortunately, I was unable to read these because they appeared, on cursory examination, to contain large numbers of words.

But I did interview the head of the Japanese F.O.E.O., which is called the Keidanren. This interview was not my idea: Hiroshi made me do it. One day he left a note at my hotel stating that he'd made an appointment for me to meet with the president and director of Keidanren, who was going to "brief" me on "Japan's economic success and the present and future Japan–United States trade relation." There was no way for me to get out of it; at that point in the trip, I didn't know how to operate the telephones.[2] Or how to scream *HELP!*

---

[2] I later learned that Japanese telephones work pretty much like ours, except that the person on the other end doesn't understand you.

Hiroshi's note said that the Keidanren is "the most powerful economic organization in Japan." I knew this meant I had to do two things:

1. Wear a tie.
2. Think up some questions.

This second item is especially important in an interview, because without questions the two of you just wind up sitting around humming. This is why real journalists always have big piles of stored-up questions ready to ask, generally involving useful all-purpose words such as "shortfall" and "infrastructure." Wake a real journalist up out of a sound sleep and thrust him into a room with, say, a U.S. senator, and without a moment's hesitation the journalist will say: "Senator, do you expect the shortfall to impact upon the infrastructure?" Then the senator will start talking and the journalist will go back to sleep.[3]

But I was having trouble thinking of questions to ask the head of the most powerful economic organization in Japan. One possibility was: "Do you think the eel shortfall will impact upon the infrastructure?" But beyond that I was pretty much stumped.

Thus it was with some concern that, on the appointed day, I put on a tie,[4] got into a taxi, and

---

[3] This is the very essence of democracy.
[4] Also pants, of course. I'm not a total farmer.

DAVE BARRY showed the driver the introductory note that Hiroshi had written for me, which looked like this:

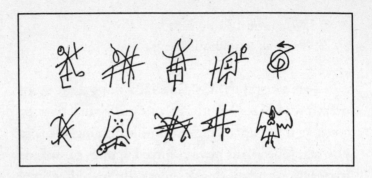

Let me tell you that it is not a comfortable feeling being in a giant incomprehensible city where you can't speak or read the language, and the only hope you have of getting to your destination and back is a small piece of paper that, for all you know, says: "I wish to fondle your pastries."

But the driver seemed to understand Hiroshi's note, and after taking the mandatory random thirty-minute route through streets and alleys and restaurant kitchens, we arrived at the Keidanren building. I showed my note to the security guard, who directed me to an office, where I showed my note to a receptionist, who directed me to a room containing a round table with a big doily on it and five upholstered chairs with several doilies each. Then she went out and closed the door.

I was alone in there for fifteen minutes, which is a long time when you are a journalistic fraud waiting to interview the head of the most powerful economic organization in Japan. The only questions I could manage to think up were:

1. What am I doing here?
2. What is it with all these doilies?

I realized that I should have done some research on Keidanren. Now, "Keidanren" is a scary-sounding name. It sounds like one of those powerful high-tech international crime operations that was always trying to kill James Bond by such means as shooting poison darts out of trick brassieres worn by attractive women. It occurred to me that at any moment the door could burst open and a sneering man, surrounded by burly uniformed guards, would march in and say: "So, Mr. Barry, you wish to speak to the Leader? I would be *happy* to arrange that, but first, in accordance with ancient Keidanren tradition, you will fight Rex the Giant Abalone. *Seize him, men!*"

Fortunately this did not happen. What happened was, a young man in a business suit came in, bowed, and gave me his card. I should explain that business cards, as you may have heard, are *very* important to the Japanese. It's not like in the United States, where the main function of business cards is so that you always have something in your wallet to pick your teeth with. Oh, sure, you can also give your cards to people, but they'll only do what you do with *their* cards, namely throw them away. Nearly 68 percent of the total U.S. landfill capacity is now occupied by business cards.[5]

But in Japan, where everybody has to know exactly where everybody fits in, who is more important than whom, who should bow the lowest, etc., the business card is a big deal. When Japanese businesspeople meet for the first time, they always exchange cards, and each one studies the other's card to see where he stands in the great pecking order of life.

So anyway, this young man handed me his card, which was in Japanese on one side and English on the other. It said he was Fumitaka Urano, Special Assistant, Office of the Chairman. So I handed him my card, which was in English on one side and blank on the other and said I was a *Tropic Magazine* Staff Writer, *Miami Herald*. We each studied the other's card. It felt kind of like the card game called "War." I thought maybe he was going to say: "OK, Special Assistant beats Staff Writer by eight points! Advantage mine!"

But instead he sat down and gave me a Keidanren brochure, which had pictures of the officers, a group of older men with expressions of stern purposefulness bordering on stomach discomfort. The brochure said: "Keidanren plays an active and influential role in the achievement of harmonious economic prosperity for all mankind."

---

[5] Source: *Sports Illustrated.*

Whoa. Harmonious economic prosperity for *all mankind*. And you thought they were just making VCRs over there.

Mr. Urano informed me that there was a brand-new Keidanren division, not listed in the brochure, called the Social Philanthropy Department. I gathered that this was a response to the often-voiced criticism that Japanese businesses don't care about social issues, or the environment. "Private companies in Japan have come to be interested in philanthropy," Mr. Urano told me. "For example, protection of the global environment."

The way he said it, it sounded like all over Japan, leading businessmen just woke up one morning and said to their spouses: "You know, I have come to be interested in philanthropy. For example, protection of the global environment."[6]

Mr. Urano and I sat for a while, pretending to be enthralled by the Keidanren brochure; then he left. A few minutes later in came the Big Tofu himself, Masaya Miyoshi, an urbane man who had been a Fulbright Scholar and spoke excellent English. We exchanged cards, and his beat mine by 680 points, but he was too smooth to make a big deal about it.

Now it was time for me to ask a question. I must say that, despite my nervousness, I was able, when the time came, to represent the journalism

---

[6] Of course this could have been confusing if their spouses didn't speak English.

profession with the cool poise and savoir-faire of a groom walking down the aisle trailing eight feet of toilet paper.

"Do you think," I said, "that, um, Japan and the, uh, United States, I mean, there's an awful lot of, you know, I mean, the *tension,* here you make all these *cars,* you know, and how come there is so much, I mean, admittedly, on *both* sides . . ."

This is only an approximation. I was actually not so coherent. Fortunately, as it turned out, Mr. Miyoshi didn't really expect to be interviewed. He expected to make a presentation on the Japanese Economic Miracle, and as soon as I shut up he launched into it.

Basically he said that Japan has been very lucky to do so well, and owes a big debt of gratitude to the United States.

"We had a very good start thanks to the guidance we got from the United States," he said. "We are the pupil who has faithfully executed what he learned from the teacher."

He said that although there have been misunderstandings between the two countries, Japan really *wants* the United States to be the world leader. The United States has had some problems, he noted, but all we have to do is restructure the economy, reduce the deficit, strengthen our industry, reorganize the educational system, reduce the crime rate, and, bingo, we'll be right back on top.

"Your goal is to guide the entire humanity," he said.

"But we don't *want* to guide the entire humanity" is what I should have said. "Why don't *you* guide the entire humanity for a while, and *we'll* get rich making VCRs?"

But I didn't say this, or anything else, because Mr. Miyoshi was in deep lecture mode, making a detailed presentation on the Japanese Economic Miracle, complete with charts. I should have paid more attention here. For all I know, he leaked important industrial secrets that I could have brought back and used to stimulate the U.S. economy to the point of orgasm. But the situation was starting to feel like Economics 101, and I could feel my brain cells sneaking out, one by one, from the lecture hall of my cranium. The only specific thing Mr. Miyoshi said that sticks in my mind is that Japanese industry and government have a "matrix." I have no idea what that means. "Matrix" is one of those words that you see around, and maybe you even *use* occasionally, but you never really have to know what it means. It's a lot like "parameter." In fact, it's quite possible that Japanese industry and government also have parameters. Somebody should look into it.

Me, I was happy to get out of the Keidanren with at least some limited ability to see through the glaze that had formed over my eyeballs. I admit that I was feeling a little intimidated by the Japanese Economic Miracle at this point, and I wanted proof that there was *something* produced in the United States that sold well in Japan. So I took Beth and Robby to Tokyo Disneyland, which has been a humongously popular attraction over there since it opened in 1983. The Japanese absolutely love it, which is weird, when you think about it.

I mean, a big reason for the success of the Disney operation in the United States is that it offes Americans a romanticized, sanitized view of their own country's past. When you enter Disney World and walk down Main Street, USA, it's as though you've gone back to the year 1910, and you're walking down the main street of a small midwestern town filled with cute stores and nice people who for some reason occasionally like to dress up as enormous rodents. You can see the appeal of this for Americans, but why do the Japanese like it so much?[7] Their Main Street looks *exactly* like the ones in the United States, with the old movie house, the penny arcade, the ice-cream parlor, and the saxophone band playing "When the Saints Go Marching In."

Oh, there were a few indications that we were not in Orlando. For example, outside the "It's a Small World After All" ride, there were Disney characters singing "Zip-A-Dee-Doo-Dah" in Japanese.[8] Also the food was different. The ice-cream parlor sold tea-flavored ice cream. In Westernland,

---

[7] Don't expect to find an answer in *this* book.

[8] The Japanese translation of the phrase "Zip-A-Dee-Doo-Dah" turns out to be "Zip-A-Dee-Doo-Dah." This remains the only Japanese phrase that I can pronounce confidently.

they sold a snack called "Tongari Corn." The box
said: "It's a Corn Snack of Crunchy Type." I ordered a "Trailblazer Sandwich," which turned out
to be tuna salad. This hearkens back to the era of
the Old West, when pioneer families were crossing
the Great Plains in covered wagons, and Pa would
grab his rifle and go out hunting for tuna.

But most of Tokyo Disneyland looks exactly
like the Disney theme parks in the United States.
And for some reason, the Japanese think this vision
of America is wonderful.

That is not, of course, how they feel about our
cars. While I was in Japan, I saw exactly three
American cars. They were all dark-blue Cadillacs.
In fact, now that I think of it, they might all have
been the *same* dark-blue Cadillac, owned by gangsters following us around because we were the only
people in Japan besides them wearing sunglasses.

But aside from that particular Cadillac, American cars do not sell at all well over there. This is
what led to the famous trip that President George
Bush made to Japan in early 1992, the one where he
led a delegation of high-level Detroit auto executives,[9] who had to be flown over in giant military
cargo jets because ordinary planes would have been
unable to lift their wallets.

The goal of this trip was to get Japan to import more American-made cars, but the U.S. dele-

---

[9] Including Lee "Air Bag" Iacocca.

gation sounded like a bunch of big fat overpaid whiners. A lot of people thought it was pretty embarrassing, seeing as how the biggest problem facing the U.S. auto industry is that a lot of *Americans* won't buy American cars. The only good thing to come out of the whole trip was when the president barfed on the Japanese prime minister, which is the kind of frank exchange that we would like to see more of between world leaders.

We also need to compete with the Japanese auto makers, which is why I asked Hiroshi Ishikawa to arrange for me to visit an auto-manufacturing plant. My plan was to pick up some valuable industrial espionage to pass along to the U.S. auto industry as a patriotic gesture and also in hopes of getting a free car.

Hiroshi arranged for me and an interpreter to visit a Nissan plant in Oppama, which is about an hour by train from Tokyo. Once again I was treated as though I were an actual journalist. I was ushered into a conference room, where I met three Nissan executives, who greeted me by exchanging "high-five" style handshakes and telling me the joke about the golfer who gets a snake bite on his penis.

No, seriously, we exchanged cards, and then the highest-ranking executive and I sat down at a table while the other two executives stood off to the side and watched us. Then the highest-ranking executive took out a piece of paper and began reading from it in a very solemn manner. According to the interpreter, he was explaining the Japanese Economic Miracle to me. He made the following specific points, which I wrote down in a official reporter-style notebook:

1. Japan has been very lucky to do so well, and owes a big debt of gratitude to the United States.
2. Japan makes a lot of cars.
3. This is accomplished via mass production.

After we got this cleared up, I asked, through the interpreter, if I could go watch them make some cars.

"Perhaps you would like to see a video first," said the executive.

This, of course, meant: "Shut up and watch the video, zitbrain."

So we watched the video, which began with the narrator saying: "Cars. What fantastic machines."

The video lasted for about twenty-five minutes, during which, according to my notes, the following points were made:

A. Nissan makes cars.
B. And darned good ones, too.
C. These are then sold to customers.

Finally the video ended and it was time to go into the manufacturing plant. This was a huge building filled with large machines making loud noises. Every few feet one of the executives would point at a machine and shout something to the interpreter, who would shout something to me, which although unable to hear, out of courtesy I wrote down in my notebook.

But I saw enough to finally figure out their secrets. Here is how they do it. First of all, they use steel. They have great big slabs of steel lying around at one end of the factory, and along the way the steel is bent into special automotive shapes until, at the other end, *voilà,*[10] it has turned into a Nissan Stanza.

But steel is only half the secret. The other half is *robots.* There were very few people along the assembly line, but there were a *lot* of really smart robots.[11] When a piece of Stanza-shaped steel came down the line, the robots would swarm all over it, waving long mechanical arms around, welding and bending and drilling and bolting. They can keep this up hour after hour, never stopping to go to the bathroom or eat lunch or gather around the coffee machine and talk about the previous night's game in the Robot Softball League. They just work. Although I suspect that late at night, when the executives go home, they loosen up a little, maybe engage

---

[10] Or, as the Japanese say, "Na-go-YAH-mah-ha-wan-ju-ka-se-MAH-na-ho-ho-wa-gah."

[11] Smarter than Tobor. Smarter, for that matter, than Captain Video.

in robot-style pranks such as welding "KICK ME" signs to each other's backs. Also on Saturday nights they probably pass around a container of gear lubricant and sing traditional robot-style blues, such as:

> My *woman treat me bad*
> *She treat me mean an' cruel*
> *Yes my woman treat me bad*
> *She treat me mean an' cruel*
> *If she don't treat me good tonight, lawd*
> *Gonna drill a .03546" hole in her main control*
>   *module*

Anyway, the point I want to make is that if we want to have a Japanese Economic Miracle here in the United States, we need to get hold of some of these robots. Maybe we could trade baseball players for them. Then all we need to do is get some steel, give it to the robots, and bingo, we'll be cranking out competitive cars like nobody's business. Of course these cars would be Nissan Stanzas, but so what? If the Japanese don't like it, they can sue us. They might have robots, but we have *way* more lawyers.

CHAPTER

6

ROCK MUSIC
IN JAPAN

*Hep Cats
Getting Funky
in Unison*

I will admit to a serious prejudice against the popular-music scene in Japan, because Japan is responsible for what is probably the most reprehensible technological development in the history of music—more reprehensible than the automatic disco-beat machine; even more reprehensible, if you can conceive of such a thing, than the amplified accordion. I am referring to karaoke.

The term comes from two Japanese words, "kara," meaning "amateurs," and "oke," meaning "getting up in bars and singing for your entertainment until you want to punch them." This technological feat is accomplished by means of a machine that plays the music to popular songs while displaying the lyrics on a screen, so that people can get up, grab the microphone, and display their singing talents. Except that, as you have probably noticed in your everyday life, most people don't have a whole ton of singing talent, which is why they have to get real jobs.

Nevertheless the Japanese are fond of going to bars where they pay good money to get lit up and inflict bad singing on each other. One of the most popular karaoke tunes is "My Way," which has been proven, in U.S. government studies, to be the most obnoxious song ever written.[1] So I think we can all agree that karaoke is a bad thing that ought to be prohibited except in special circumstances, such as when I personally wish to sing.

I did this one night in Tokyo with some other trained professional journalists when we went to a karaoke bar after eating at a restaurant where, at

---

[1] Consider these lines:
Regrets? I've had a few.
But then again, too few to mention.

BARRY the end of the meal, they served us sake in a box. It was a big box o' sake, is what it was.

> ## IMPORTANT TRAVEL ADVISORY
> ### NEVER DRINK SAKE OUT OF A BOX. OR ANY OTHER WAY.

So we got to this karaoke bar, and we ordered what the menu described as "Bad Weiser Beers." Then we were given a list of the karaoke-machine songs, which included not only rock and pop tunes, but also that spiritually moving traditional Christmas favorite, "Away in a Manager." The lyrics were also listed. In case you have always wondered what the words are to the chorus of Paul McCartney's "My Love Does It Good," here they are:

> *Woe woe woe woe*
> *Woe woe woe woe*[2]

For a while we just drank our Bad Weisers and watched the other bar patrons perform. A tiny middle-aged woman got up and sang the Louis Arm-

---

[2] These words are the registered copyrighted trademarked patented property of Paul McCartney Worldwide Enterprises Corp. Inc. Ltd. and may not be reprinted, reproduced, rebroadcast, memorized, sung, hummed, or in any way enjoyed without the express written consent of about twenty-seven lawyers, who, frankly, have no intention of returning your phone call.

strong version of "Summertime," and she sounded *exactly* like Louis Armstrong, right down to the scat parts. It was eerie—as though Louis Armstrong had never really died, but instead had entered the U.S. government's Satchmo Relocation Program and emerged from extensive cosmetic surgery as a very petite Japanese woman. Or maybe that was just the box o' sake kicking in.

Then, as is required by the Japanese constitution, a man got up and sang "My Way."

Next up were one, no, two American men, who attempted to sing "Mack the Knife." It started out as just one guy, but then another guy, recognizing the song, thought he'd give the first guy a helping hand, so he weaved up to the microphone and started pitching in. The first guy, feeling that he did not need any help, repeatedly shoved the second guy away, but the second guy would merely weave around in a crooked circle and head back toward the microphone. By the second verse it was getting to be more like Roller Derby:

There's a [shove] ("OOF!") tugboat
Down by the—MOVE, DAMMIT!—river . . .

After a few more performers had appeared, my group decided that karaoke was the stupidest, most pathetic excuse for entertainment we had ever seen, and we wanted to become part of it. So we selected a song and told the master of ceremonies to

115

announce the name of our group, which was embarrassingly juvenile and tasteless and need not be repeated here.[3]

Besides me, the group consisted of reporters for the *Wall Street Journal,* the *Washington Post,* and *Newsweek.* The song we performed was "My Boyfriend's Back," which in 1963 was a big hit by The Angels, and which begins:

> *My boyfriend's back, and there's gonna be*
>   *trouble*
> *(Hey la, hey la, MY BOYFRIEND'S BACK!)*
> *If I were you, I would cut out on the double*
> *(Hey la, hey la, MY BOYFRIEND'S BACK!)*

We gave the song a strong effort featuring coordinated hand gestures, and I feel we did an excellent job of representing our country in the sense that none of us actually fell down. The audience watched in deeply impressed silence. "Always be an ambassador of goodwill wherever you go" is one of my mottos.

One of the cultural ambassadors singing the "Hey la, hey la" part that night was Paul Blustein of the *Washington Post,* who told me that if I wanted to see the *real* cutting-edge music scene in Japan, he'd take me to Harajuku, a park in Tokyo where, on Sunday afternoons, Japanese rock bands gather to perform for their fans. So one Sunday we

---

[3] Tom and the Tampons.

went there, and I was very glad that we did. Although there may be vast cultural differences between Japan and the United States, the scene in Harajuku served as heartwarming proof that rock music is indeed the universal language of the young, and the Japanese young cannot speak it worth squat.

I admit that I am not exactly Mr. Happening Dude in the music department myself. I am definitely stuck in the sixties. I hate heavy-metal bands with shrieking men in Spandex. I hate rap music, which to me sounds like a bunch of angry men shouting, possibly because the person who was supposed to provide them with a melody never showed up. In the car, I listen to radio stations that play Golden Oldies, and I sing along with genuine emotion when the song asks:

> *Who put the bomp in the bomp ba bop ba*
> *bomp?*
> *Who put the dip in the dip da dip da dip?*[4]

Also, one time I actually danced to the song "Bad, Bad Leroy Brown." This occurred at a wedding reception, but that is still no excuse. I am not cool, and I know it. I am an out-of-it, middle-aged suburban person whose idea of a wild evening's activity is filling out the warranty registration for

[4] Copyright © 1962, Joyce Carol Oates.

his Water Pik. But after seeing what passes for hipness in Harajuku, I felt like Jimi Hendrix. I felt cool enough to be on the cover of *Rolling Stone*.

I started feeling this way the instant we arrived, because the first thing we saw was the Bad-Ass Greasers. These were young men, maybe a dozen of them, deeply into the 1950s-American-juvenile-delinquent look, all dressed identically in tight black T-shirts, tight black pants, black socks, and pointy black shoes. Each one had a lovingly constructed, carefully maintained, major-league caliber 1950s-style duck's-ass haircut, held in place by the annual petroleum output of Kuwait. One of them had a pompadour tall enough to conceal former President Carter.

For a while the Bad-Ass Greasers just stood around combing at their hair and looking as sullen and rebellious and James Dean–like as possible. Then they formed a circle and sat down cross-legged, like people gathering around a campfire. One of them turned on a boom-box cassette tape of "Heartbreak Hotel." The circle started clapping to the music; one of them got up, went to the middle of the circle, and began dancing. The dance he chose to do was—get ready for the epitome of menacing Badness—the Twist. He did it stiffly, awkwardly, looking kind of like Steve Martin and Dan Aykroyd doing the wild-and-crazy-guys routine, except that he was deadly serious. So were the guys clapping in the circle. They clearly believed that they were too hip for mortal comprehension. They did not seem to sense that they might look a little silly, like a gang of Hell's Angels that tries to terrorize a small town while wearing tutus. Americans in the onlooking crowd would periodically catch each other's eyes and have to turn away. (We are famous for our good manners.) But the Bad-Ass Greasers were oblivious. Convinced of their coolness, they clapped and twisted grimly on.

And in a way they *were* cool, compared with the other groups I saw in Harajuku. Playing loudly on both sides of the street, for a hundred yards or so, were twenty or so rock bands, each of which had come with a truckload of instruments, sound equipment, and generators. They had set up within a few feet of each other, and they were all playing simultaneously, so it was impossible to hear one without hearing several others. No harm done.

They were uniformly awful. It was the Festival of the Bad Loud Semituned Bands Doing Lame Imitations of MTV Stars. But what was really pathetic about them was their desperately misguided effort to be *different*. For example, you don't see a lot of tie-dyed T-shirts in Japan, and there was one band whose members all wore tie-dyed T-shirts, which I guess made them different by Japanese standards, but they all wore virtually the *same* tie-dyed T-shirt. And dancing in front of them was a crowd of groupies—all teenaged girls, and *they* all wore the same shirt, on top of which they were all

DAVE BARRY doing the *same dance step*, which I assume they thought was cool, but which I swear looked exactly like the "Hokey-Pokey."

And a few feet away was a band whose members wore plaid, and of course their fans wore plaid, and they had their own dance, which was basically the "Jerk." And in a few more feet there was a band with purple hair, and then one that wore leather, and so on, each band with its official look and its groupies wearing their official groupie uniforms and dancing their official dances and glancing sideways at each other to make sure they were all being different in unison. It was sad, really. All these kids, gathered in one place, trying *so* hard to be rebellious and iconoclastic, while in fact being far more regimented than a typical American bowling league.

But I can't say that I felt depressed. In fact I felt wonderful, after being so intimidated by the industriousness, competence, and rapid technological progress of the Japanese, to discover that there is a Hipness Gap, a gap between us so vast that their cutting-edge young rockin' rebels look like silly posturing out-of-it weenies even to a middle-aged dweeb like myself. They buy our music, they listen to our music, they play our music, but they don't *get* our music. I admit that I don't either, much of the time, but at least I'm hip enough to know it.

Which is not to say that there's nothing we can learn from them. As we were leaving, we

120

passed a young, innocent-looking schoolgirl groupie leaning against a yellow band van with a big sign proclaiming:

> KING
> FUCKER
> CHICKEN

Which you have to admit is a good new name for a band.

CHAPTER

7

HUMOR IN JAPAN

Take My Tofu!
Please!

I've been concerned about the humor situation in Japan for some time, because humor is my business, and in any business you have to be alert to the possibility of foreign competition.

Of course, most Americans do not think of Japan as a humor-intensive, wocka-wocka kind of nation. The way Americans see it, if the nations of the world were a high-school class, Japan would be the nerdy little kid in thick glasses who always sat in front and never screwed around and turned in thirty-seven extra-credit reports in color-coordinated binders. We don't look to Japan for humor, a fact that is reflected in our economy: Currently, only .08 percent of the humor consumed in the United States is imported from Japan.[1]

But that's exactly the situation we were in with automobiles thirty years ago, and *now* look at us. My big fear is that even as you read these words, technicians in Japanese humor laboratories are analyzing older Woody Allen movies, using sensitive instruments to determine *exactly* what is funny about, for example, the scene in *Everything You Always Wanted to Know About Sex (But Were Afraid to Ask)* wherein Woody gets chased across the field by a female breast the size of a Taco Bell.

Using this knowledge, and aided by a new generation of powerful, sophisticated, humor-generating computers such as the YUK-3000X, the Japanese could be developing advanced new consumer-friendly, easy-to-tell jokes with punchlines that work every time. They could be preparing to flood the American market with vast quantities of cheap, reliable laughter, which would put thousands of American humor workers out on the

---

[1] Source: The U.S. Commerce Department, Division of Statistics, Bureau of Small Percentages.

street, where they would have to eke out a precarious living by shouting insults at pedestrians. It could get ugly. Innocent people could get hit by pies.

I don't want to see my child grow up in a country like that, not with the high cost of dry cleaning. So when we got to Japan I was determined to find out what the Japanese humor industry was up to.

Not much, was my immediate impression. By Western standards, the Japanese are subdued in public; I hardly ever heard anybody laughing out loud. I did see a lot of comic books, which are a huge industry in Japan, but most of them are not meant to be humorous. They're more like novels or action-adventure series with pictures, and they tend to contain a lot of violence and sex. Several times, riding in the Tokyo subway, I'd be standing next to a middle-aged businessman in his business suit, and he'd have a fat comic book, which he'd be frowning at studiously, as though it were the Third Quarter Sales Trends, and I'd glance at the page he was looking at, and there would be a naked woman with hooters so large that I half expected to see a little cartoon Woody Allen running away from them.

This struck me as odd, because I think of Japan as a much more restrictive place than the United States, yet you never see American businessmen commuters openly reading sex comics. They all have their heads buried in the *Wall Street Jour-*

nal. It makes you wonder. Maybe, if you manage to penetrate the *Journal*'s dense protective layer of 158 pages of tiny sleep-inducing numbers about mayonnaise futures, you get to a lurid full-color comic feature entitled *Throbbing MBA Lust Members*. Maybe this is one of the secrets they teach at Harvard Business School.

But in Japan the sex comics are right out in the open, which bothers a lot of people, because the plots often involve rape and other forms of sexual violence against women, including schoolgirls. Yet the incidence of real sexual crimes in Japan is way lower than it is in the United States.

And there's another paradox to ponder. Sexually explicit material is readily available in Japan, and there are many "massage parlors" and sex shows. Of course I personally did not attend any of these shows, due to a combination of being extremely moral and traveling with my wife. But I spoke with a journalist who had attended one with a group of other journalists for sound journalism reasons, and he said it was quite explicit.

"A woman did the most incredible thing with her vagina, a yo-yo, and some fruit"[2] were his actual words.

So there's a sex industry operating quite openly in Japan, yet at the same time there are censorship laws that seem prudish by U.S. stan-

---

[2] No, I'm not going to tell you what.

dards. For example, they don't allow pubic hair. I mean, they allow it on *people,* but they don't allow it on *pictures* of people. If you buy an American edition of *Playboy* magazine in Japan, you'll find that somebody has gone through it with a sharp implement and *scratched out all the pubic hair.* I'm serious. Open the magazine up to the Playmate of the Month,[3] and she'll be striking a sultry and seductive pose, but her personal region will have this little *cloud* over it, as though a key reproductive organ has caught fire, or she has encountered some kind of unusually small, low-lying storm system.

"Hey!" she's thinking. "It's raining on my privates!"

There are little clouds over *everybody's* privates in magazines in Japan. The government employs people who spend their days going through magazine after magazine, scratching out pubic hair, spending their days in the universe of crotches. I wonder what THAT job would be like. I wonder if the employees talk about their work at lunchtime. ("Do you BELIEVE Miss October?" "No! I'm wearing out blades like crazy! She looks like she's being attacked by a wolverine!")

But my point, to the best of my recollection, is that comic books are not really a humor medium in Japan. There are humorous shows on Japanese television, but the ones I saw looked like copies of

---

[3] *Name:* Krystal. *Turn-on:* Working out. *Turn-off:* Words with syllables.

American shows, or actually were American shows. For example, several times I saw the show *Alf*. It had been dubbed into Japanese, but I could follow it anyway, because there was a laugh track to let you, the audience, know whenever Alf said anything funny, which of course was every time Alf said anything. To me he seemed just as funny in Japanese as he did in English. Funnier, in fact. My son and I found ourselves watching the show with exactly the same fishlike stares we have when we watch TV in English.

If you've watched enough television in your life, you don't *need* to understand what they're saying. You can still grasp the basics. On the Japanese news, if the announcers had happy faces and perky voices, I knew that meant good news, such as that Japanese scientists had discovered a way to make VCRs even more difficult for Americans to program; whereas if the announcers had serious voices and frowny faces, it meant bad news, such as a worsening of the eel shortage. On the quiz shows, if the contestants looked sad, it meant they had lost; if they laughed and wept and joyfully embraced like people who had just been miraculously cured of cancer, it meant that they had won golf clubs. It was just like at home.

If you pay attention, you can even understand Japanese soap operas. I found this out one day in Hiroshima when we were eating lunch with an interpreter. We were in a tiny restaurant serving a cuisine called *okonomi-yaki,* where you sit at a

DAVE BARRY long hot griddle, and the cook whips up a large pancakelike affair with noodles, cabbage, pork, and many other things, then squirts some Worcestershire sauce on top and slides it over to you, and you eat it right off the griddle.[4]

Over the griddle was a TV, which was showing a soap opera featuring a woman packing some clothes and talking to two children. My wife, Beth, who does not look at soap operas in America, watched for a moment, then, to the amazement of the interpreter and me, started explaining what the woman was saying:

> BETH: She's telling them that she has to leave for good.
> INTERPRETER: That's right!
> BETH: She says it's better for them this way, because she and their father don't get along.
> INTERPRETER: Yes!
> BETH: She's telling them that they will have to be strong.
> INTERPRETER: Exactly!
> BETH: She says they must be the women in the family now.
> INTERPRETER: How are you *doing* this?
> BETH: Oh, you can just tell.

So it is possible to bridge the gap between the two cultures. You can do this with soaps, and Beth,

---

[4] Or, if he slides it all the way *into* your lap, you scream and never have children again.

128

but I don't think we're going to do it with humor. I base this statement on our experience with Japanese stand-up comedy.

Actually, they don't stand up. They kneel. It's kneel-down comedy. It's called *rakugo,* a medium in which the performer tells humorous stories, many of them traditional. As far as I could tell, it's the closest thing they have in Japan to our comedy clubs.

We went to a *rakugo* performance in the company of a superb interpreter named Itsuko Sakai, who learned English as a girl when she lived in the United States for several years. She said that when she returned to Japan, the adjustment had been difficult for her, because she'd acquired some American mannerisms. "In Japan," she said, "if you look Western, it's OK for you to be different. People expect it, people will help you. But if you look Japanese, and you don't *act* Japanese, people can be really cold."

Itsuko said she did a lot of interpreting for heavy-duty government agencies involved in technical matters such as international fishing-treaty negotiations. She wasn't sure how well she'd do translating *rakugo* humor, but she agreed to take a stab at it.

The performance took place at a small theater; the stage was bare except for a pillow with a microphone in front of it. Beth, Robby, and I sat together near the back, and Itsuko sat one row behind us, leaning forward so she could whisper the translation to us. We were the only Westerners there. The audience was very quiet, as Japanese audiences tend to be. There was no alcohol being served, and there were of course no hecklers. People did laugh from time to time, but often long minutes would pass during which they'd just sit there, looking serious, like witnesses to an autopsy, while the performer told his stories. If an American comedian got that kind of crowd response, he'd slit his wrists by the third joke.

Itsuko labored mightily to give us the play-by-play, but most of the time we were totally lost. The performers tended to tell long, wandering stories, often taking five minutes to set up a punchline, which would turn out to be impossible for us to understand because it involved a play on words, or a knowledge of written Japanese. Sometimes Itsuko didn't get the joke. Sometimes *nobody* seemed to get the joke. Many stories seemed to be random collections of statements beamed down from Mars. After a while we found ourselves laughing just because we weren't getting anything.

Anyway, I took notes as fast as I could, and so, ladies and gentlemen, without further ado, let me bring out for your entertainment . . . my notes from the *rakugo* concert! Let's give them a warm Chapter Seven welcome!

(APPLAUSE.)

Thank you. So first this young guy comes out

and kneels on the pillow. He says he's a student of

rakugo, and he fires off these two one-liners about his teacher:

1. "My teacher likes baseball, and often he uses the rice spoon for a bat."
2. "He likes baseball so much, he calls us dead balls."

The audience members do not laugh, but the young man compliments them for being a good audience anyway. He then notes that when you compliment people, you should keep your jaw down low, because if you keep your jaw up, it doesn't sound like you're complimenting. He demonstrates this technique.

Then he does a long word-play joke about sake, involving a lot of dialogue like this:

"I hear you had free sake."

"But it's not free sake."

"You should give me some compliments."

"Well, what should I say?"

"Say my shop is clean."

"OK, your shop is clean."

This goes on for several minutes, during which the audience displays no more reaction than a pile of gravel. Suddenly the dialogue turns to babies:

"I hear you got a new baby."

"Yes."

"The child is bald and wrinkled. He must have had a hard life. I can even see traces of a mustache."

"That's the grandfather."

We Americans laugh here, but nobody else does. Maybe they've heard it. The dialogue continues:

"Here's the baby! When I press the stomach, it cries."

"Stop pressing! You'll kill the baby!"

This appears to be the end of the joke, but nobody laughs here either. Eventually a new guy comes out. He's a little older. He sees us in the audience.

"We have foreigners here," he says.

We nod.

"They're nodding," he says. Then he launches into a long story about being asked to go to a job interview at a magazine. Here's a summary of the story:

When the guy got to the job interview, there were three beautiful women in high heels.

They asked him to take a shower, so he did.

Then they tied him up. "I felt like a roast beef," he says.

Then they walked on him in their high heels.

Then they handcuffed him.

Then they tried to put him on an X-shaped rack, but he wouldn't fit.

So they brought a lit candle near him, and he stretched out and fit.

End of story.

We are mystified. Itsuko is mystified. The audience is absolutely silent. So far about twenty minutes of comedy have elapsed, and there hasn't been one outright laugh, except ours, at the wrong time.

The next performer is an eighty-year-old man who uses a violin bow to play music on a saw.

"I haven't always been old, but I've been alive for eighty years," he says. This gets a laugh.

"When I was young," the man continues, "I used to sing the blues in the rain. So now I'm going to use the saw to play the blues."

He plays a tango on the saw. It was as fine a tango rendition as I have ever heard on a saw. The audience gives the man a nice hand.

Then a younger performer comes out. He tells a joke that gets the biggest response of the evening so far. Here it is, in its entirety:

"It has been very hot. Two days ago I ate too much sushi." Pause. "Now I'm not feeling well."

Next he tells some jokes based on the names of commuter train lines around Tokyo. One of these is a bathroom joke, based on the fact that the station's name also means "wiping with paper."

The next joke gets a big laugh:

"The signs in other train stations say 'Show Your Commuter Pass.' The signs in my train station say: 'You should not lend your commuter pass to other people.'"

He also gets a big laugh with this:

"I'm facing this way because I see another balding man. You see we have the same head."

A new performer comes out. He says that when women drown, their bodies float faceup,

133

whereas men's bodies float facedown, "because they have a weight."

"So they found a body floating sideways," he says. "Turns out he was gay."

(*LAUGHTER.*)

His next story concerns an old man who passes a restaurant where a cook is about to kill an eel. The old man feels sorry for the eel, so he buys it from the cook and throws it into the river, saying, "It's a lucky thing I passed by, eel!"

The cook, realizing this is a good way to make money, makes a point of having an eel on the chopping block every day when the old man comes by; the old man always buys and releases it. But one day the cook has no eel, so when he sees the old man coming, he picks up a baby, claiming that a customer has ordered it. The old man, shocked, buys the baby.

"It's a lucky thing I passed by, baby!" he says, and throws it into the river.

(*BIG LAUGH.*)

Then another guy comes out and tells the longest joke in the history of the world, consisting of a dialogue between two bums:

"Why don't we have some sake?"

"We don't have money."

"Why don't we get some?"

"Where?"

"In the bank."

"You have money in the bank?"

"I don't. Other people's."

"I'd like to go to a place where you don't need money, but I don't have enough money to travel there."

Fifteen minutes and approximately two audience chuckles later, the story begins to near its climax, which involves the question of whether the bums will eat some tofu that they got the previous day. The bums discuss this and discuss this. The audience listens patiently, absolutely stone-faced. An old man two rows behind me is snoring loudly. The dialogue, as Itsuko whispers in our ears, is taking on a surreal quality:

"Two or three days ago it was very hot."

"Are you in a hurry?"

"I'm in a hurry, but I'm not rushing."

"What about the tofu?"

"It looks terrible. It looks like the back of a shirt."

So at this point, along comes an uppity guy, and the two bums show him the sour tofu.

The uppity guy says: "It's amazing that you were able to get hold of this. Among us gourmets, this is very famous."

And then he *eats it!* Ha-ha! Get it? The uppity guy *eats the sour tofu.* Is that a killer story, or what?

Well, it got a HUGE laugh from the *rakugo* audience. Bigger than the one for the baby-into-the-river story. Even the snoring man woke up and laughed.

So there were definitely some thigh-slappers,

135

but basically I came away feeling a lot less worried about the potential Japanese threat to the U.S. humor industry. Japan clearly is still a long way from developing the kinds of sophisticated humor mechanisms that we Americans enjoy, such as rim shots, booger jokes, and the House of Representatives. We are so far ahead, in fact, that I think we should make a concerted effort to reduce our trade deficit by exporting more American humor products to the Japanese market, starting with the ones that are easily adapted to foreign cultures:

> FIRST JAPANESE PERSON: Wah ga no SAH ma ha no ga mah?
> SECOND JAPANESE PERSON: Nah ha mah go wah sa NAH mah ha. [*Pause.*] NOT!!

SPORTS IN JAPAN

"Yo, Batter!
Loudly Make It Fly!"

When we think of Japanese sports, we immediately think of sumo wrestling, an ancient, tradition-rich sport played by superb athletes who prepare via a strict centuries-old training regimen of eating 275 quarts of Häagen-Dazs butter pecan per day.

And even that much ice cream doesn't seem

like enough caloric input to account for the fat buildup on these athletes: I suspect that some of them are surgically enhanced. It would not surprise me to learn that cosmetic surgeons in the Los Angeles area are saving the fat that they remove from their patients via liposuction, then selling it to Japanese corporations, which ship it in converted oil tankers across the Pacific to Japan, where it is injected into sumo wrestlers via a process called "lipopumping" that basically involves changing the setting on the liposuction machine from "SUCK" to "BLOW."[1]

The reason why these wrestlers need to carry so much weight is that they want to look as attractive as possible in their traditional fighting uniform, which is in essence a very large jockstrap. Ask any leading fashion consultant, and he or she will say, "Oh, yes, there is nothing more appealing, from a visual standpoint, than a man who carries an extra two hundred or three hundred pounds who is naked except for a jockstrap with a thin strip going up the back, thereby permitting personal hairs and butt cheeks the size of the Lincoln Memorial to hang out over all Creation."

Yes, sumo wrestlers are definitely a visual treat. You have to look quickly, however, because the matches don't last long. Under the rules of sumo, two wrestlers get into a small ring, and the

---

[1] Warning: Do not try this at home.

first one who can knock the other one down or shove him out of the ring is the winner. This usually takes no more than a few seconds, and then both wrestlers are free to leave and replenish any fat cells they may have lost during their ordeal. So we are not talking about a sport with a whole lot of action. A major sumo championship match, comparable to the seventh game of the World Series, is generally over in less time than it takes a single American baseball player to adjust his protective cup on national television.

I don't see sumo catching on in the United States. Americans are accustomed to having their major sporting events presented in the form of massive-overkill TV extravaganza productions such as the Super Bowl. This approach would not work well with a sumo championship match, given its extremely short duration:

ANNOUNCER: And so, as Wayne Newton, the Boston Philharmonic, and the world-famous Rockettes conclude that stirring fourteen-minute rendition of the national anthem, culminating in the first Space Shuttle launch ever attempted from inside a domed stadium, we come at last to the end of our pre-match show, which, as you may recall, began at 4:00 P.M. yesterday.

FIRST COLOR MAN: That's right, Jim. The time for speculation is over, and now it's finally time for these two great sumo wrestlers to get

139

into that ring and decide once and for all who is number one.

SECOND COLOR MAN: That's right, Norm and Jim. And we have a capacity crowd on hand for this long-awaited event, as we can see from this overhead shot from our exclusive Rafter Cam.

THIRD COLOR MAN: That's right, Norm, Jim, and Ted, and as we can see in this close-up shot from our exclusive Hot Dog Vendor Cam, these fans, like our millions of viewers around the world, are charged with excitement in anticipation of this much-anticipated event.

FOURTH COLOR MAN: That's right, Norm, Jim, Ted, and Bob. These fans are not about to leave their seats for any reason, as we can see from this shot of a completely empty stadium men's room, taken from our exclusive Urinal Cam. And so as we prepare—

SECOND COLOR MAN: *Uh*-oh.

ANNOUNCER: What?

SECOND COLOR MAN: I'm looking at the guys down in the control truck, via our exclusive Guys Down in the Control Truck Cam, and they're holding up a hand-lettered sign that says: "They just fought the match, you cretins."

ANNOUNCER: Well, maybe we can catch up with these two great wrestlers in the locker room via our exclusive . . .

No, sumo is never going to be big in America. Nevertheless it is a sport that involves tremendous strength, agility, skill, cunning, and strategy, and it is fascinating to watch. In all fairness, I should note that I am lying. Sumo looked to me like two severely porky guys in jockstraps lunging into each other for about three seconds and then calling it a day. But so many people seemed to be so riveted by it that I figured I must be missing something.

I saw some of Japan's top wrestlers perform, thanks to Hiroshi Ishikawa, of the Foreign Press Center, who took me to a sumo exhibition on the grounds of a junior high school in a small town called Otombecho, about ninety minutes north of Tokyo by train. It was a glaringly hot, humid day, but the exhibition was a big deal, a local holiday, and thousands of people had come. Wearing long pants or dresses, they sat patiently for hours under the blazing sun on blankets—there were no chairs—around the wrestling ring.

Most of the wrestlers waited in the school gymnasium until it was their turn to wrestle. Then they'd head for the ring, moving with a ponderous, waddling gait caused by the fact that they had thighs large enough to affect tides. These were enormous men, looking like a different species from the typically small, slim civilian Japanese, who stepped aside and stared at each wrestler as he passed through the crowd, moving like a rhinoceros scattering a flock of birds. Hiroshi and I also stared as a vast man, looking as though he could easily weigh four hundred pounds, waddled past.

"Now you wonder how we lost the war," Hiroshi said.

Before each match, the two opposing wrestlers always perform an ancient traditional ritual involving clapping their hands, throwing some salt into the ring, squatting, and raising their legs sideways one at a time, then stomping them down, as though killing ancient traditional cockroaches. This ritual is extremely traditional and richly symbolic, and it is also so comical-looking to the uninformed Western eye that I would probably have laughed out loud were it not for the fact that the men performing them could have, merely by sitting on me, turned me into a flat, uninformed reddish ground smear.

After the ritual, the two wrestlers step into the ring and engage in a display of tremendous strength, agility, skill, cunning, and strategy, cleverly disguised as two overweight men lunging together, and one of them almost immediately pushes the other out of the ring. Then the fans express their appreciation for the winner via a display of wild enthusiasm, Japanese style, which means they got about as loud and rowdy as a lone American gargling.

Some of the wrestlers, when their matches were over, would waddle over to the vendors and, mingling with the fans, get food and drinks. I thought this was pretty neat. It was as if you were

at, say, a pro football game between the Chicago
Bears and the Detroit Lions, and afterward an of-
fensive tackle, in uniform, showed up at the re-
freshment stand. I watched one sweating wrestler
accept a can of soda from a vendor, tilt his head
back, and swallow all of it in one gulp, then let out
a burp that caused surfable waves of fat to ripple
across his massive belly. It was a Diet Coke.

Nearby was another vendor standing behind a
table covered with a mound of odd-looking red-
dish-pink snakelike things. I moved closer and discovered that these were tentacles. Which you were
supposed to pay for and then *eat*. I stared at them
with undisguised horror, which amused the vendor, who said something to me, then grabbed a
handful of tentacles, shoved them into his mouth,
and started chewing. He was laughing while he
chewed, and the end of one tentacle was sticking
out of his mouth, wriggling around, as though he
had a live squid in there.

Still chewing, the man picked up a tentacle
and thrust it at me, shouting something. A small
crowd was now watching us.

"He wants you to try it," said Hiroshi.

"Go ahead," said my wife, whom I used to
trust.

"Yeah, Dad! Try it!" said my son, who is so
picky about his *own* food that he will eat only
certain parts of a pizza slice.

Thus, feeling intense group pressure, I put the
tentacle into my mouth and, tentatively, chewed. *143*

And although as you have already gathered I am not a big fan of exotic foods, I have to tell you in all candor that it was truly awful. The best way I can think of to describe the sensation is: It's like chewing on a squid tentacle, only somehow worse. It occurred to me that if I swallowed it, there was a chance that the suckers could spontaneously activate and latch onto my esophagus wall halfway down. Gagging, I staggered over to a garbage can and spat out the tentacle, while the vendor and the crowd enjoyed a hearty laugh, as did my son, who will not receive a penny in my will.

So anyway, I can't say that I'm hot to see any more sumo wrestling. Nor am I a big fan of another sport that is hugely popular in Japan—namely, golf. In many cities we saw high-rise, multitier driving ranges, often right downtown, with giant nets around them to keep balls from flying out and killing the general population. We also saw commuters practicing their swings (without clubs, of course) on train platforms. And we saw golf equipment and apparel for sale everywhere. The Japanese eat, sleep, and breathe golf; the only thing they don't do is actually *play* it, because to get on a course, you have to make a reservation roughly 137 years in advance, which means that by the time you actually get to the first tee you are deceased. Of course, in golf this is not really a handicap.

I realize that golf is also wildly popular in the United States, a fact that totally mystifies me, inasmuch as a round of golf offers essentially the same

degree of action and excitement as trying to find
your car in an airport parking lot, except that golf
is physically less demanding inasmuch as you ride
in a little cart. Nevertheless I have noticed that, as
I get older, golf has claimed more and more of the
guys I know at work. One day they're regular guys
who enjoy real sports such as basketball and football and trying to hit selected coworkers with rubber bands, and the next day they're talking about
how they bogeyed their par wedges with a four-
iron. They can't remember the ages or even necessarily the names of all their children, but they can
drone on in great detail about exactly what happened on every golf hole they ever played. It's scary
to watch this happen to somebody you thought you
knew. It's like in the movie *Invasion of the Body
Snatchers,* when the beautiful heroine thinks she's
the only human left on earth whose body has not
been taken over by the evil Pod Things from Space,
and she sees Donald Sutherland and goes up to him,
overwhelmed with joy at finding that she is not
alone, only to recoil in terror when he tells her, in
the film's shocking finale, that he has decided to
change his putting grip.

So I didn't play golf in Japan. But I did watch
some baseball, which has been a major sport over
there for a long time. One of Japan's most-followed
sporting events is the annual high-school baseball
tournament, which was going on when we were
there, and which people were watching on tiny
portable TVs everywhere we went. One Saturday

Tom Reid of the *Washington Post* took me to one of the semifinal games in a Tokyo stadium between Kugayama High and Kogaguin High. There was a good crowd on hand, with the adults conservatively dressed and the students all wearing uniforms and standing in their official cheering section.

Cheering is very much a designated group activity at Japanese sporting events. It's not like in the United States, where every fan feels free to exercise his right, as spelled out in Article VI of the Constitution, to root for his team in the manner reflecting his own individual and unique feelings, the result being that you hear a wide variety of cheers, ranging all the way from calling the umpire an asshole to calling the umpire a dickhead.

But at Japanese baseball games, the crowd is, much of the time, eerily silent. The fans will applaud a good play and occasionally make some group noise, but you virtually never hear a lone voice yell or heckle. Such a display of individualism would be highly embarrassing in Japan, in stark contrast to America, where a person who can yell clever insults at sporting events may well receive movie offers.

In Japan, the cheering is done by specific groups standing in specific areas and performing precise, unvarying cheer routines, which are repeated over and over and over and *over*. At the high-school game, each side's official rooters

cheered only when their team was batting, and
remained politely silent when the other side was up.

Tom and I sat near the Kugayama High students—the boys in dark pants and white shirts, the
girls in the sailor outfits favored by Japanese
schools. Following the direction of some boys in
front holding up signs, the students would yell the
appropriate cheer. When a batter was up, they invariably yelled, *"Kato ba se!"* Tom told me that
this meant, literally, "Loudly make it fly!" It was
translated more colloquially in his Japanese-
English dictionary as "Deliver a homer!"

There was also a band and a group of male
cheerleaders who wore black pants, Kugayama
T-shirts, samurai-style headbands, and white
gloves. Every few minutes the band would strike up
the Kugayama High fight song, and the cheerleaders would thrust out their fists and do a little dance
step that looked sort of like old-fashioned boogie-
woogie and sort of like the hora. What made this
especially entertaining to watch was that the
Kugayama High fight song was, for some reason,
set to the tune of "Popeye the Sailor Man." And
what made it even better was the fact that the
opposing Kogaguin High anthem was set to the
tune of—I swear—the Mickey Mouse song.

So what you had was two groups of highly
enthusiastic students, cheering for the honor of
their schools, and when the game would reach a
crucial moment, one side would be thrusting fists

147

and shouting with samurai intensity to the accompaniment of a song that to Western ears is inextricably linked to this stirring message:

> *I'm Popeye the sailor man!*
> *I'm Popeye the sailor man!*
> *I'm strong to the finish*
> *'Cause I eat my spinach*
> *I'm Popeye the sailor man!*

And then the other side, showing its proud fighting spirit, would come back with the Mickey Mouse Club song, hearkening back to the ancient days when brave samurai warriors roamed the land and, in epic battles that have long been recounted in traditional Japanese literature and song, attempted to knock the officially licensed Walt Disney World souvenir mouse-ear hats off their enemies' heads.

The game itself was somewhat less exciting than the cheerleaders. The Japanese, Tom told me, tend to play conservative baseball. In this game, nobody ever tried to stretch a single into a double, even when the chances looked pretty good. When a runner got on base, the next batter invariably bunted, regardless of the score. There were quite a few base runners, but not one steal attempt. Needless to say there was also no dancing, taunting, gesturing, posturing, or trick handshaking. When the game was over (Kugayama won), the teams lined up and bowed to each other, then toward their fans; then the Kugayama players shouted, "Banzai!"[2]

Tom and I also attended a professional baseball game, between the Yomiuri Giants and the Yakult Swallows.[3] The game was in Tokyo's domed stadium, which is called, because of its shape, "The Big Egg." Tom wore his souvenir Big Egg hat, which had the following clever word play printed on it:

Big Enter Taiments and Golden Games

We had to pay a scalper to get in, because the game was a sellout, which is normal for the highly popular Giants. But the capacity crowd was making no more noise than the one at the high-school game. All the cheering was being done by two groups of highly organized fans in their designated cheering sections on the opposite side of the stadium from where Tom and I were sitting. The people around us were stone silent. I honestly couldn't tell which team they were rooting for.

I supposed that in a way the serenity was pleasant; more than once, at sporting events in the States, I've wished that a thoughtful security guard would come along and quietly shoot a paralyzing dart into some loud spittle-emitting moron behind

---

[2] Literally, "We're number one!"
[3] If you think "Swallows" is a silly name for a baseball team, bear in mind that Hiroshima has one called the "Carp."

me. But somehow it just didn't seem right, all this silence at a sporting event. So after four innings and two beers, when a batter named Hara got up, I momentarily forgot where I was, and I said—just sort of conversationally, not yelling at all—"All right, Hara."

Do you remember that TV ad for E. F. Hutton, the one where two people are talking at a crowded party, and one of them says that his broker is E. F. Hutton, and suddenly everybody in the room stops and turns to listen? Well, that was pretty much what happened in the Big Egg when I said "All right, Hara." Literally hundreds of people whirled around to see who was making all this noise. Food vendors stopped vending so they could look at me. For all I know, Hara stepped out of the batter's box to see who was making all this racket.

"You stupid foreigner," said Tom, helpfully. "That's not even an official cheer."

Fortunately the crowd saw that I was just an out-of-it clod, so I wasn't asked to leave or anything. This meant I was there when a Giants player hit a home run, which meant that I got to see the traditional home-run ritual, which consisted of a girl coming out of the dugout and presenting the player with: a doll. Really. I have no idea why this is done, but it makes a nice little tableau: Mr. Hero, holding this doll, while the fans applaud in unison. But I doubt you could

bring this ritual to American professional baseball
and our sporting tradition. If a little girl attempted to hand a doll to an American player,
he'd probably take a swing at her. And the fans
would boo if he missed.

CHAPTER

9

STAYING AT A JAPANESE INN

Peace, Tranquillity,
Insects

After a week in Japan, we decided to leave Tokyo and spend some time in a traditional Japanese inn, just the way vacationing Japanese do, except of course that they do not make total dorks of themselves at every possible opportunity.

We started doing this right away at the train

station. Trains run everywhere in Japan, and they run *exactly* on time—we took dozens, and not one was even a minute late. So we had to be there on time, but we had a hell of a time figuring out where "there" was. Usually we had reserved-seat tickets, which meant we'd have to get to the right station, then get to the right platform, then get to the right position on the platform, then get into the right car, then find the right seats. All of these numbers were on our tickets of course, but sometimes the words—like "car" or "train number"—were in Japanese only, so basically I was looking at a piece of paper covered with assorted marks and numbers, like a lottery ticket from Mars. Also most of the station signs were in Japanese. Also hardly anybody in train stations ever spoke English. It was like a national policy or something.

So we were never calm in the stations. I was the least calm, feeling that I was supposed to know which way we were supposed to go. This is of course classic Guy Behavior. You take a man and a woman, knock them both out with chloroform, put them into an airplane, fly them to South America, and leave them in the heart of the Amazon jungle in the middle of a starless night without a compass, and the instant they wake up, the man will announce: "We want to go this way."

So we'd be lugging our luggage through a crowded, bustling station, with me leading the way, frowning at the tickets, trying to decide whether we wanted Car 9 of Train 17 on Track 3, or Car 3 of Train 9 on Track 17, or possibly even Car 17 on March 9, and I'd announce, "Up this stairway!" And Beth would say, "Are you sure?" And I'd say "Of COURSE I'm sure," in the irritated, superior manner characteristic of a guy who is lost.

So we'd struggle up the stairs, and I'd lead us to where I thought we should be on the platform. I'd keep sneaking glances at the tickets, just in case I had suddenly, without realizing it, acquired the ability to read Japanese. And then a train would come, and since it was at the right time, I'd figure it had to be the right train, so I'd say "Let's go!" And Beth would say: "Are you sure?" And I, very irritated now, would say: "YES! GET ON THE TRAIN! IT'S GONNA LEAVE!" Because the trains do not wait around in Japan.

So we'd pile all our luggage on, and there would be a conductor, and Beth would say, "Maybe we should ask him if this is the right train," which would REALLY tick me off, the implicit suggestion being that I didn't even know which train we were on, which of course I didn't. So I'd reluctantly show the conductor our tickets, and he'd shake his head and point across the platform to *another* train, and I, continuing to take charge, would say, "GET OFF THE TRAIN! IT'S GONNA LEAVE!"

Then we'd grab our bags and struggle off and lunge across the platform and get on the other train, where we'd of course discover that we were at the extreme opposite end from where our seats were. So we'd have to lug our luggage through car after car after car—I suspect that prank-loving Japanese railroad workers were actually adding cars to the train as we went along—until finally we'd reach our reserved seats, usually at just about the same time that our train reached its destination.

Using this technique we traveled westward from Tokyo to Kyoto on one of the famous bullet trains, which get their name from the fact that they are shaped like giant sex appliances. These trains reach speeds of well over one hundred miles per hour, and I have been told that they are very comfortable if you ever locate your seat. Also there are men's rooms with urinals and convenient windows on the doors so that people walking past in the corridors can look in, apparently to determine whether the room is occupied. I found this out by accident when I went into one of these rooms and closed the door behind me, without noticing the window. I was facing the wall, engaging in standard rest-room activities, when I happened to glance around, assuming that I would see a nice, solid, totally opaque door, and instead—*YIKES*—I saw three schoolgirls about eighteen inches away, causing me to whirl back toward the wall and become grateful that I was wearing dark pants, if you catch my drift.

Other than that we had an uneventful ride to Kyoto. Hurtling along, I noted that most Japanese cities seem to be smaller than Tokyo, but just as

DAVE BARRY ugly. I also noted that virtually every city and town, even the small ones, had at least one large, modern, usually garish pachinko parlor. Pachinko is a popular gambling game; you pay money for a bunch of little balls, which you put into a contraption—kind of like a vertical pinball machine—that buzzes and beeps and flashes and zings the balls all over the place. By skillfully doing something with a knob—I never figured out what—you can win *more* balls, which you can then exchange for prizes.

Robby and I played pachinko once, in Tokyo, in a noisy, brightly lit room full of serious-looking, chain-smoking, suit-wearing men manipulating the machines with the obsessed, joyless, I-need-a-life look you see on the faces of people cranking Las Vegas slot machines. Robby, who has a black belt in video games, instantly comprehended the game and started winning balls. I had no idea what I was doing with my machine. It had an electronic picture of a large-breasted woman on it, and the balls would bounce around her, and every now and then she would suddenly start to remove pieces of her electronic clothing.

"Hey," observed Robby, staring at his machine, which was making a lot of noise, "you can get it so her clothes come all the way off."

"We have to go now," I said.

Aside from pachinko, I also noted, on the train ride to Kyoto, that Japan contains both agriculture and geography. I'll have more on both of these topics if I become truly desperate for material.

When we arrived in Kyoto, we took a cab to our inn, which was a traditional type of Japanese inn called a *ryokan*.[1] When we pulled up in front, three women in kimonos came out and began bowing and saying things in Japanese and picking up our luggage. Using our Japanese skills, we said "thank you" or possibly "good night," and we bowed, and they bowed some more, which was not easy for them to do while holding our luggage, and then we started to go into the inn, at which point the women started speaking excitedly and pointing at our shoes.

Japan has a thing about shoes. You can wear them into stores and westernized hotels and restaurants, but you're not supposed to wear them into homes or traditional inns. You're supposed to take your shoes off at the door and put on slippers. And then if you go to the bathroom, you're supposed to take off *those* slippers and put on *another* pair of slippers, which are just for the bathroom. This custom may seem silly, but there's a sound reason for it: It keeps foreigners confused. At least that's what it did for us. I was always forgetting to change footwear, plus the slippers were always too small for me, so to keep my feet in them, I had to kind of mince around.

Following the baggage-carrying *ryokan* ladies, I minced with Beth and Robby to our room,

---

[1] Literally, "type of inn."

which was in the very simple, very beautiful Japanese style, everything in light-colored wood. There was a sliding paper screen that opened up into a little cicada-infested rock garden with a brook babbling through it. The room had no beds or bureaus or chairs, only straw floor mats and a low table. In a *ryokan,* when you want to sleep, a maid comes in and puts down some futons for you. In fact, the maid comes in a lot; you got the feeling she was always just outside the door, day and night, ready to come in and do something for you. Our maid, who was wearing a kimono and a beeper, came in about thirty seconds after we arrived, speaking in the high, singsong voice that Japanese women often use when they're speaking to somebody in authority.[2]

"*Hai domo!*" she said.

She said "*Hai domo!*" to us a lot. As far as I was able to determine, "*Hai domo!*" means "Yes, very!" We came to think of her as the Very Lady.

She gestured to indicate that we should kneel with her around the low table, then she welcomed us to the *ryokan* via a nice little traditional ceremony wherein she poured us some tea and served us some kind of mysterious green substance. We smiled and bowed and drank the tea, and we each ate about one molecule of the green substance, and we smiled some more to indicate that it was the

[2] This drove Beth *crazy.*

best darned mysterious green substance we had ever eaten and we would almost surely be wolfing it down later on.

DAVE BARRY DOES JAPAN

Then the Very Lady showed us, via ancient traditional *ryokan* hand gestures, how to operate the TV remote control. She also showed us the bathroom, which was, like the rest of the inn, done in the beautiful, simple Japanese style, with lots of light-colored wood, accented by a Woody Wood-pecker hand mirror.[3] The maid also showed us our *yukata*, which are lightweight bathrobelike garments that you're supposed to wear while you stroll (or, in my case, mince) around the *ryokan*. The idea is that you become extremely relaxed and contemplate the rock garden and listen to the brook babble and the cicadas chatter until you achieve total inner peace. Or, if you are a typical hyperactive American suburban mall-oriented family like us, you go stark raving mad.

Maybe the problem was that the cicadas went off at about 4:30 A.M. and apparently had gotten hold of small but powerful amplifiers. So between them and the sudden unexpected appearances of the Very Lady, we never got quite enough sleep in the *ryokan,* plus we never experienced the total relaxation that comes from taking a traditional Japanese hot bath. The Japanese like to soak in

---

[3] Here is another interesting *ryokan* bathroom fact: There was never any shampoo, but every day there were three new toothbrushes.

wooden tubs filled with extremely relaxing water hot enough to melt Formica; this is one of the first things you're supposed to do when you get to the *ryokan*. I almost did this the first evening. I minced down the hallway to the bath area, and I started to go in, and although there was a lot of steam in the air, I was able to determine the following:

1. There were people in there.
2. I did not know these people.
3. These people were naked.
4. These people represented all of the major genders.

So I minced the hell out of there and back to our room, where I contemplated the beauty and natural wonder of people speaking Japanese on television.

That evening we wandered around downtown Kyoto, looking for a restaurant that might have some form of local food that our son might eat, such as Ring Dings. We'd been in Japan for over a week, and we were starting to feel the strain of hardly ever being able to understand people or read signs or know for sure whether the dish we had just pointed to on the menu was going to arrive with live gasping sea cucumbers in it. And now we were in Kyoto, which is less westernized than Tokyo, and we were staying in a small, terminally peaceful inn where the main form of entertainment was insects, and we were feeling down. I realize that this was our fault, for being too stuck in our American ways to be able to adapt to another culture, but I bet there were times when even a great traveler like Marco Polo just wanted to find a cheeseburger and a Holiday Inn, and this was one of those times for us.

So we were feeling depressed and lonely as we walked the streets of Kyoto, looking at plastic food. We finally went into a restaurant and ordered what turned out to be food that none of us really liked, which was OK inasmuch as most of it ended up on my shirt due to the fact that at this point I was committed to learning how to use chopsticks.

TRAVEL TIP:
HOW TO USE CHOPSTICKS

Take one chopstick and place it between the base of your thumb and your hand, extending outward between your middle and ring fingers. Grasp the other chopstick with the tips of your thumb and index finger. Now, holding the two sticks parallel, raise them over your head and signal to the waiter that you would like him to please bring you a fork.

So we were all still hungry when we left the restaurant. We each wandered along in a lost and lonely waiflike manner until Robby spotted a sign that said: PIZZA. (Robby, standing on the Earth, could spot a pizza sign on Neptune.) So we went into a little store and got a large pizza. We carried it outside and sat in a small park next to a temple, and even though the pizza had corn on it, we wolfed it down. Passing pedestrians stared at us, three foreign water buffalo feeding in the wild.

Our mood improved vastly the next day when we toured the Kyoto area with Kunio Kadowaki, a warm, mellow, and funny man who has worked with many journalists on assignment for magazines such as the *National Geographic*. He was born in Kyoto in 1942; the first Americans he met were GIs.

"They gave me some chocolate," he said. "My father worked fourteen hours a day, but we never had chocolate."

He took us first to the Shimyoin Buddhist temple, way, way up a winding, narrow road in the rugged, heavily forested mountains above Kyoto. There are temples all over Japan, and visiting them is a major tourist activity for both the Japanese and foreigners. Many of them are lovely, but my feeling about temples is pretty much the same as my feeling about important cathedrals in Europe, which is that after you've seen a representative sample of them—say, two—it's time to move on to other major tourism activities such as lunch.

But the Shimyoin temple, far off the beaten tourist path, was worth the visit. It's a small, simple building set in the densely wooded hillside next to a spring, from which flows a mountain stream that eventually joins with others to become the river that flows through Kyoto. We were greeted at the temple by the priest and his wife, who invited us inside to have tea and cookies in a room overlooking the stream and the valley. The priest, a friendly and cheerful man, spoke a tiny bit of English, but we really didn't have to say much; we mainly just sat there and enjoyed our tea and watched the water flow off down toward the city.

This turned out to be Kunio's method of being a tour guide: He'd take you to some quiet, beautiful place, tell you a little about it, and then shut up and let you experience it. Kunio radiates mellowness rays. After a few hours with him our antsyness was gone. We'd often just sit and look and think, with nobody speaking for minutes on end. Even Robby.

From what I gathered, religion is a fairly casual thing in Japan. The major religions are Buddhism and Shinto, which coexist cheerfully, with most people choosing to believe elements of each as the need arises. There doesn't seem to be much in the way of rigorous dogma or strict priestly authority; it's more of a hang-loose, do-it-yourself deal, wherein if you want to do well on an exam, or heal an illness, you go and make an offering, or waft some incense smoke over the afflicted area. At the larger temples you can also buy fortunes and charms. In one Tokyo temple, I bought a charm for Traffic Safety; I figured this would be useful in Miami, where there are drivers who will attempt to pass you inside a car wash.

I like the relaxed way in which the Japanese approach religion. I think of myself as basically a moral person, but I'm definitely not religious, and

I'm very tired of the preachiness and obsession with other people's behavior characteristic of many religious people in the United States. As far as I could tell, there's nothing preachy about Buddhism. I was in a lot of temples, and I still don't know what Buddhists believe, except that at one point Kunio said: "If you do bad things, you will be reborn as an ox."

This makes as much sense to me as anything I ever heard from, for example, the Reverend Pat Robertson.

Kunio took us to some other lovely temples, but our favorite excursion, two days later, was when he took us back into the mountains for one of the most breathtaking drives I've ever seen, on a hairpin-turn mountain road about as wide as a paper towel through steep, heavily wooded mountain canyons with straight, tall cedars all around us, sunlight filtering through from way up, bouncing off green mountainsides, and a sparkling stream. We passed through a few small villages with thatched-roof houses, but, despite the fact that this was vacation season and Kyoto wasn't far away, we saw only one or two other cars. In the United States, such a spectacular drive would be bumper-to-bumper with tourist cars. Kunio said the Japanese prefer to go on package tours to major sites; the road we were on was inaccessible to buses.

Kunio also took us to what was, for Robby, the ultimate shrine: the headquarters of the Nintendo company. For the benefit of those of you who live on Mars without children, I should explain that Nintendo is an extremely popular video game that modern youth learn how to play while still in the womb. The way it works is, you hold a little control box that's connected by a wire to the Nintendo unit, which is connected to your TV set. By pressing various buttons, you control a little cartoon character on the TV screen.

In most Nintendo games, the character you control is trying to survive in a world filled with deadly dangers and an endless supply of bad guys and evil creatures trying to kill him. It's a lot like New York. But your character has various skills and weapons, and by pressing the buttons in a certain manner, you can cause him to get killed immediately. At least that's what happens whenever *I* play. I'm so bad at Nintendo that my character, when he realizes who's controlling him, will sometimes pull out a cartoon razor blade and slash his own wrists. But when Robby controls the character, he is invincible. If Robby didn't have to quit for bedtime, his character could not only kill all the bad guys but also significantly reduce the federal budget deficit.[4]

As far as Robby's concerned, Nintendo is Japan's most significant cultural contribution to the world, and when we were over there he was constantly going into electronics stores to look for

---

[4] At least he would definitely come closer than Congress has.

advanced Nintendo technology. Stores in Japan have a lot of electronic gadgets not available in the United States, and Robby had read in a video-game magazine that there was a new device, called Genie, that enabled you to give your Nintendo character important new powers. He had looked for it, without success, in store after store in Tokyo. When he found out that Nintendo's headquarters was in Kyoto, he was determined to go there and see if they knew about Genie.

Kunio said that when he was a boy, Nintendo was just a small company that manufactured playing cards. Now it's a big international business. I wondered if the headquarters would somehow reflect the product that had made the company so successful—like maybe when you walked in, giant hostile turtles would rush up and kill you unless you jumped on their backs and turned them into empty shells (this is typical of the feats your Nintendo character must perform). But the Nintendo building looks sternly businesslike and non-fun-oriented—a gray building with a security guard post outside and a stark, modern lobby.

Nevertheless the receptionist was receptive when Kunio explained that Robby was a serious Nintendo player on a mission. She asked us to wait in the lobby, which we did for several minutes, during which I tried to calculate how much of the building I, personally, had paid for via excursions to Toys "R" Us. About two-thirds is what I figured.

ing fish using cormorants, which are a type of musical instrument similar to the trumpet.

No, just kidding. Cormorants are a type of aquatic bird sort of like pelicans. They're used in a centuries-old nighttime fishing technique still practiced in a few places, including a town near Kyoto called Uji. We took a train out there one evening, and found it to be a pleasant little river village, nice and peaceful except for a man at the train station shouting angrily over a huge truck-mounted public-address system. That's what political activists do in Japan: They shout angrily at you over powerful amplifiers turned up loud enough to pulverize concrete. As a persuasive technique, this leaves much to be desired. We saw quite a few of these trucks in Tokyo, and nobody paid any attention; everybody just walked briskly past.

This is smart. If you stood still and listened, you'd be deaf as a tire iron within minutes. So if the activists ever *did* attract any followers, they'd have a hell of a time carrying out whatever political actions they had in mind:

"WE MUST STRENGTHEN OUR MILITARY!"

"WHAT DID HE SAY?"

"HE SAYS HE WANTS TO LENGTHEN OUR CAPILLARIES."

"NO, THANKS, I ALREADY ATE."

Anyway, we walked briskly away from the angry shouting man at the Uji station, and I asked a pedestrian for directions, using the international symbol for cormorant fishing, which is when you have one hand pretend to be a cormorant and swoop down on the other hand, which is pretending to be a fish.

He aimed us toward the river, where we found fishermen preparing some long, narrow wooden boats. At the end of each boat was a pole sticking out over the water; suspended from this was a wire basket in which the fishermen had built a log fire. The purpose of the fire is to attract the fish, although why a creature who lives under water would be attracted to fire is beyond me. Perhaps these are unusually stupid fish.

When night had fallen and the fires were burning brightly, the fishermen brought out some baskets, three per boat, each one containing two cormorants. The men put leashes around each bird's neck, looped so that the bird could get a fish into its mouth but not swallow it. Then the men pushed off from shore and started drifting down the river, two men controlling each boat and a third man in front, near the burning basket, holding leashes attached to the six cormorants, who swam around and squabbled with each other.

At first this approach didn't look terribly practical; my impression was that it would be a lot less trouble to try to scoop up the fish with trumpets. But it turned out that the cormorants, once they stopped squabbling, did a pretty good job. They'd disappear under water, and every third or fourth time they'd come up with a fish. Whenever this happened, the leash man would haul the cormorant in, snatch the fish away, and shove the cormorant back out. You'd think eventually the cormorants would get ticked off about this, maybe start plotting acts of revenge ("Watch this! I'm going to bring up a used condom!"). But I guess the cormorants aren't a whole lot smarter than the fish.

Still, it made for a pleasant evening's diversion, a uniquely Japanese experience, and we were in a good mood as we headed back to our little Kyoto *ryokan*, with its peaceful babbling brook and its cheerfully chattering cicadas. Someday I will go back and kill them with a flamethrower.

C
H
A
P
T
E
R

10

HIROSHIMA

Before I got there, the only thing I knew about Hiroshima was that we had dropped an atomic bomb on it. For me, Hiroshima *was* that menacing mushroom cloud. I expected it to be a mournful memorial city, perpetually wrapped in gloom, a place where every activity would be dampened and shadowed by the terrible

173

thing that had happened there. I wondered if its residents would despise me, maybe confront me angrily, for having the insensitivity to come to a place where my country had caused so much pain.

But life, as has been noted, goes on. And it has definitely gone on in Hiroshima, which is, on the surface anyway, an ordinary, busy Japanese city, with stores and streetcars and gardens and temples and an old castle for tourists to visit.

The atomic bomb, too, has become a kind of tourist attraction. Visitors get their pictures taken standing in front of various bomb-related sites and memorials; the people—especially the younger ones—are often smiling, sometimes laughing, like tourists standing in front of the World's Largest Ball of Twine.

We chose to be in Hiroshima on August 5, the anniversary of the attack. Along with thousands of other visitors, we attended the annual memorial ceremony, held in the morning, when the bomb had dropped. On our way in, some Boy Scouts gave us flowers to place on the memorial to those who died. The crowd—around us, anyway—seemed quite cheerful. Our interpreter, Yuko Yamaoka, told us that the anniversary activities have taken on an almost festive tone over the years. She said that many A-bomb survivors resent this and no longer attend the public events, preferring to hold private services.

There was an unusually large contingent of media people on hand for the ceremony, because news was going to be made: The mayor of Hiroshima, in his official Peace Declaration, was going to include, for the first time, a brief statement acknowledging Japan's guilt for the suffering it had caused in Asian countries during World War II.

Japan, as you surely know, has been much criticized for allegedly failing to take responsibility for its actions before and during the war. Critics charge that Japan has tried to position itself as a victim, forced to fight in self-defense against racist Western nations that would never allow Japan to achieve its rightful place in the world. Critics also charge that the Japanese tend to equate the bombing of Hiroshima with the attack on Pearl Harbor, the two events canceling each other out, leaving neither side holding the moral high ground. These are still very sensitive topics in Japan, and the debate continues to rage between those who want Japan, the land of harmony and nonconfrontation, to confront its history, and those who see no point in dredging up all this nonharmonious unpleasantness, fifty years later.

But the dropping of the A-bomb is definitely, and understandably, remembered in Japan. The problem, for some, is *how* it's remembered and its historical context or lack of it. In *The Enigma of Japanese Power* (a book that has been sharply criticized in Japan), Karel van Wolferen argues that Japan disregards the historical events that led to the atomic attack, preferring instead to wallow in self-pity and victimhood:

It has become common in Japan to consider the dropping of the atom bomb as the worst act of the war. Some even see it as the crime of the century. Older Japanese still have some sense of perspective concerning these events. A few will remember that, before Hiroshima was devastated, the generals had formed a civilian militia of 28 million men and women between fifteen and sixty years of age, who were being trained to stop the U.S. invaders on the beaches using only bamboo spears. But a Japanese intellectual or public figure can no longer suggest with impunity that the bombs probably saved hundreds of thousands of lives. And for a week in August the nation indulges in a media-generated display of self-pity. The "peace park" and museum in Hiroshima—pilgrimage centre for numerous foreign anti-nuclear activists and pacifist groups—do not give the multitude of Japanese visitors any impression that history began before the bomb.

This is why it was considered newsworthy that the mayor of Hiroshima, Takashi Hiraoka, acknowledged Japanese guilt in his Peace Declaration during the memorial ceremony. The translation of his speech said:

Japan inflicted great suffering and despair on the peoples of Asia and the Pacific during its reign of colonial domination and war. There can be no excuse for these actions. This year marks the fiftieth anniversary of the start of the Pacific War.

Remembering all too well the horror of this war, starting with the attack on Pearl Harbor and ending with the atomic bombings of Hiroshima and Nagasaki, we are determined anew to work for world peace.

The ceremony was held outdoors in Peace Memorial Park, near the center of the blast zone. We sat with the crowd on folding chairs, facing the Memorial Cenotaph, which contains the names of the bomb victims. A stage had been erected for dignitaries and speakers; we listened through earphones to a running translation. For me, the most moving moment came at the beginning—the ritual offering of water by representatives of the victims' families. After the bomb blast, many of the dying cried out constantly for water—*mizu*—but there was none; now, finally, they receive it.

It was a hot, still morning. It became almost unbearably still at eight-fifteen, when one minute of silence was observed, during which you could imagine the sound, precisely forty-six years earlier, of a B-29 droning overhead. Then a bell tolled, the mayor gave his Peace Declaration, and some doves were set free.

Until then the ceremony had been simple, brief, and powerful. Then the politicians spoke, five of them, including the prime minister, Toshiki Kaifu. Five men in virtually identical dark suits giving virtually identical, mechanical, banal speeches. All of them were sorry, from the bottom

177

of their hearts. All of them offered their condolences to the victims' families. All of them hoped this would never happen again. All of them were for peace.

I guess all politicians, from all over the world, attend some school where they learn how to reduce anything—*anything*—to verbal sludge. Granted, it has to be difficult for politicians to talk about Hiroshima, because what can they say?

So maybe they shouldn't say anything.

After the ceremony we moved forward with the crowd toward the cenotaph, where we left the flowers that the Boy Scouts had given us. I wanted this to be a moving moment, but it wasn't, at least not for me. The crowd was packed together, with people jostling, talking, shoving forward. It was like exiting from a basketball game. I thrust my arm forward through the crowd, put my flowers down, and turned away.

We also went into the memorial museum. Some of the exhibits are scientific, explaining how hot the atomic fireball was, how big the blast area was, how the radiation sickness advanced, how many people died. But the most powerful exhibits are intensely personal: charred clothing; twisted eyeglass frames; a dark human shape on some granite steps, caused when a person's body blocked the blast rays, a shadow of death.

I found myself weeping, out of sorrow and helplessness and guilt. But I also felt anger. Because

the way the museum presents it, the atomic bomb

was like a lightning bolt—something nobody could foresee, and nobody could prevent. It was as though one day, for no reason, the Americans came along, literally out of the blue, and did this horrible thing to these innocent people.

I don't know if it's possible to justify what happened to Hiroshima—I certainly wouldn't try to justify it to the victims' families. But I found myself wanting to shout to the other museum visitors: Do you know WHY my country did this? Do you wonder what would make a civilized country do such a thing? I'm not sure that *I* know the answer, but the museum doesn't even address the question. And I don't think that just saying "No more Hiroshimas" over and over again, like a mantra, is enough to guarantee that it will never happen again.

That evening we returned to the Peace Park to watch the candle boats—little paper boats, thousands of them, floating down the river, each carrying a lit candle, symbolizing a victim. It's a lovely sight, and it drew a huge crowd, in a fine mood; families were talking and laughing, kids were racing around, vendors were hawking shaved ice cones and glowing plastic bracelets. It was a carnival atmosphere. You could see that, in another fifty years, this anniversary will have lost all its meaning, the way that for many people in the United States, Memorial Day means nothing more than picnics and softball.

I didn't want this. I wanted Hiroshima to be

DAVE BARRY reverent that night, or introspective, or even angry. Anything but festive.

Of course it doesn't matter what I want. Nobody I know suffered here. I have no right to tell the Japanese how to remember Hiroshima. And of course there's no way I could know what each person along that river was thinking, watching those little flickering candles drift toward the sea.

CHAPTER

11

IN THE COUNTRYSIDE

Tourists in Hell—
Make That Eight *Hells*

A
fter we were certain that we had seen every temple and shrine in Japan at least four times, we decided to branch out a little and visit another popular type of tourist destination, the world-famous Mikimoto Pearl Island.[1] This is

---

located in a seaside resort town called Toba, which you can easily reach by train, but don't ask me how. We followed our usual carefully planned procedure, darting nervously and randomly around train stations, looking for signs in English, and growing increasingly irritable with one another until we finally lunged aboard what could easily have been the Prison Express for North Korea.

Once aboard the train we attempted to locate our stop using the Earnest and Zippy method. Earnest and Zippy are our dogs. When we're home, we occasionally take them along in the car on some errand. They love this, because it gives them a chance to protect us by barking at dangerous menaces such as UPS trucks, other dogs, trees, lawns, etc. The problem is that they have no way of knowing when they're going to get to go for a ride. We go out the front door many times a day, and any one of these times could be the big moment. So the dogs remain on Red Alert status, monitoring our activities constantly. Whenever we open the door, they stop whatever important task they're performing, like licking the spot on the kitchen floor where somebody dropped spaghetti two years ago, and come rushing toward the door in Full Emergency Bark mode, ready for action.

"NO!" we tell them, closing the door. They generally hit it headfirst at about forty miles per hour, then bounce back, unharmed, ready to try again the next time, because you just never know.

This is basically how we located Toba. Whenever the train pulled into a station, we'd become extremely alert, pressing our noses against the window and whimpering, looking around frantically for some indication that this might be Toba. Finally, after many stops, we came to one that just felt right to us, plus there was a sign that said: TOBA. We became so excited when we saw this that it was all we could do to keep from making weewee on the floor. And it was definitely worth the effort to get there. I would say that Mikimoto Pearl Island is the finest bivalve-related tourist facility I have ever toured. It's named for a man named Kokichi Mikimoto, who died in 1954, but not before figuring out how to make oysters produce pearls in large quantities. Until then pearls had been a fairly low oyster priority.

There's a large museum on Mikimoto Pearl Island featuring exhibits that tell you in elaborate science-fair detail about how to get oysters to make pearls. Basically, you take an oyster, you open it up—something that I, personally, would never have the courage to do—and you put a small irritating particle next to the oyster's gonads. Yes! Unlike, for example, the U.S. Senate, oysters have gonads! This would suggest that they can have sex, which is amazing when you consider that (a) they keep themselves locked inside those shells, and (b) they are basically nothing more than repulsive undersea wads of phlegm.[2]

---

[2] I would no more eat an oyster than a squid tentacle. And you can quote me.

Anyway, when you insert the particle, the oyster forms a pearl, possibly because it has more time on its hands, due to the sudden reduction in its sex life. ("Not tonight, dear. I have an irritating particle next to my gonads.")[3]

Besides explaining how pearls are formed, the Mikimoto Pearl Museum provides valuable consumer information about pearls, such as:

- "They are things of beauty and give pleasure."
- "They're something people want to own; they're something people want to wear."

If I were to try to summarize, using my understanding of the nuances of Japanese civilization, the subtle underlying message of the Mikomoto Pearl Museum, I would say that it is: "Buy pearls." There is a convenient gift shop.

The museum also has a section devoted to the women pearl divers of old. Women did the diving because it was believed—this is true—that women have bigger lungs.[4] Here are some quotations from the women divers' exhibit:

. . . radiant ama [women divers] of Shima, of whom much has been sung from ancient times, are living with praiseworthy courage, ever arouseing your traveling propensity.

---

[3] Thought: A good name for a football team would be "The Cincinnati Oyster Gonads."

[4] We now realize that this is ridiculous. Right?

The art of diving they have mastered is a
trousseau they are very proud of.

Outside the museum is a grandstand where
you can sit and, at regularly scheduled times, watch
women divers, wearing what appear to be hospital
gowns, swimming around in dark-green water, diving down and coming up with oysters, which they
drop into wooden tubs, which are then hauled
aboard a boat, and then, I assume, dumped back
into the water so that the next group of tourists can
watch the divers find them. I cannot say that these
divers looked radiant. I would say they looked
cold.

On the train home from Toba, a boy about
Robby's age sat next to Robby and practiced his
English. He established that Robby was fine, and
that he was fine. They were both fine. They established this several times, and Robby gave the boy
some pretzels. As the train reached his family's
station, the boy's mother came up and gave Robby
a wrapped present (it was candy). The Japanese are
very big on giving presents.

We really didn't need candy; what we needed
was for them to tell us what station to get off at. But
it was a nice gesture, and eventually we found our
way home. We were getting better at finding our
way around without ever really knowing where we
were. The art of finding our way around we had
mastered is a trousseau we were very proud of.

If you're wondering how the little boy's

mother managed to procure a wrapped gift box of candy on the train, the answer is that she got it on the train. Food is for sale everywhere you go in Japan, including trains and train stations. And it's not just your standard mass-transit crud either, like the Nachos of Death they serve at U.S. airport and bus station snack bars, or those bloated greasy mutated pontoon-sized orange-colored hot dogs that have been rotating since the Great Depression on those automatic grilling devices. Has anybody ever actually *eaten* one of those hot dogs? Probably if you tried to, the hot dog would leap off your bun, snarling, and crawl back to join its friends on the grill.

But the road food in Japan, even in small-town train stations, is excellent—all kinds of little delicacies, very fresh, attractively arranged in little boxes. It's hard to figure how the Japanese stay so slim. Maybe it's from constant bowing.

You also find vending machines everywhere in Japan. You'll be in a dark, out-of-the-way neighborhood, on a rural mountain road, and suddenly you'll come upon a bank of elaborate, high-tech, swoopy-looking vending machines that, if they were in the United States, would long ago have been vandalized and shot and stabbed and possibly sexually assaulted.

These machines sell cigarettes, candy, coffee, tea, all kinds of soft drinks, and—this was a wondrous discovery for me—beer. If you have enough change, you can get a *giant* can of beer from some

Japanese vending machines. I'm talking about a can so large that if you bought two, you'd need to find a vending machine that sells forklifts so you could get your beer home.

For research purposes I purchased a fair amount of beer from Japanese vending machines. All of it was fine, but my favorite brand was Suntory Beer, because the labels say "Inexplicably Delicious."

Robby became addicted to a popular Japanese soft drink called Pocari Sweat. Really, that's the name. My guess is it was the winner of a national contest for Best Soft-Drink Name Involving a Bodily Fluid, narrowly edging out Pocari Postnasal Drip and Pocari Festering-Wound Discharge.

I think Pocari Sweat was supposed to be good for you, because at one point I saw a vending machine sign that said, "Pocari Sweat contains the following positively charged ions," followed by as impressive a list of positively charged ions as I have ever seen in a soft drink, and I include Yoo-Hoo in that statement.

The Japanese drink a lot of semimedicinal beverages; stores sell all kinds of potions for various ailments. At a busy Tokyo commuter station we stopped at a store with a sign that said: ENERGY POOL (FOR YOUR HEALTHFUL LIFE). The shelves were lined with hundreds of little bottles containing various-colored liquids; commuters would dash in, buy one, swig it down, and dash out.

I bought a product called Hugo, and all I can

say is, it had better be healthful, because it tastes like coyote spit. Another potion came in three types: Daily Work, Hard Work, and After Work. Beth bought Hard Work, which she thought tasted pretty good, despite the label.

> NEO URBAN REFRESHMENT
>
> TYPE 2: WHEN PHYSICALLY OVERWORKING
>
> FOR LIFE IN THE FAST LANE
>
> UCC WORKS IS AN ESSENTIAL SUPPLEMENT
>
> FOR PEOPLE LIVING IN THE MANIC PULSE
>
> OF THE CITY.

Speaking of sweat, we finally got around to taking real Japanese hot baths. We did this in the seaside resort town Beppu, where we stayed at the amazing Suginoi Hotel and resort and bath complex. This is not an easy complex to describe. Picture a major Las Vegas hotel, except that instead of a huge, garish, tasteless casino, there are huge, tasteless, garish baths. That's right: People go there on vacation, in large numbers, *to take baths*. It's difficult for us Westerners to conceive of a lavish resort centered on an activity that we view as an act of personal hygiene. It's as though you were driving along the strip in Vegas, and you saw a giant flashing neon sign that said:

The Grand Palace of Dental Flossing

> *Big Ed's Nose-Hair-Removal World*

But the Japanese really like their baths, as a way of relaxing from physically overworking in the fast lane in the manic pulse of the city. And as far as I'm concerned, taking baths is not nearly as stupid a way to spend a vacation as, for example, gradually feeding 652 pounds of quarters into a slot machine.

Which is not to say that I had a totally relaxing time in the Suginoi Hotel. I became mildly nervous moments after we checked in, encountering a sign in our room that said: "If an earthquake occur, follow the instruction of the broadcast." Call me a pessimist, but I did not think that the instruction of the broadcast would be in English.

Beppu is not an English-intensive area. As far as we could tell, we were the only non-Japanese in the hotel. This made us something of a tourist attraction ourselves, especially when we donned our resort wear. We had noticed that many of the other guests were walking around wearing their hotel-supplied *yukata,* or lightweight cloth robes. This looked pretty comfortable, so we decided to put on our *yukata,* too. But as it turns out, you're not supposed to just wear your *yukata* any old way, as though it were a bathrobe. There are *yukata* rules: Depending on your gender, you're supposed to

191

have a certain side overlapping, and tie your sash in a certain way. To get it wrong is sort of like walking around with your pants on backward.

We didn't know these rules, so we just did the best we could, but whatever we did, it was wrong. When we passed people in the halls, they'd stare and point at us, giggling and whispering to each other. Sometimes they'd burst right out laughing. This kept happening, and I never did figure out why. Perhaps I had selected the particular *yukata* setup favored by transvestite sex-change cow molesters. Whatever it was, I came to feel quite self-conscious about it, although I tried to look as unconcerned and dignified as possible, which was not easy inasmuch as I was wearing hotel slippers designed for a much smaller person, possibly a fetus, and therefore I was mincing a lot.

Footwear etiquette was a major problem for us. In some parts of the Suginoi complex you could wear shoes; in some parts you had to wear slippers; and in some parts—I think this had something to do with the baths—you had to wear a *different kind* of slippers. I never got it right. I'd be mincing along, *yukata* flapping, and I'd cross some invisible slipper frontier, causing hotel employees to rush up to me, point to my slippers, and lead me over to an area where I'd have to pick out some new slippers, which of course were *always* smaller than the ones I had on. It was the old Shrinking Slippers Trick. I bet they were secretly videotaping me for a popular TV comedy show called *Foot Fun with*

Foreigners, seeing if they could eventually get me to go around wearing condoms on my big toes.

But being hardy cultural pioneers we kept on mincing, changing footwear every few feet, until we had explored the entire Suginoi complex. It's quite elaborate, with game rooms, restaurants, a wide range of food stands, a theater, many gift shops, and a bowling alley, all gathered around two huge bath complexes. Each complex is restricted to one gender only, with the genders switching each day.[5] Fortunately this was explained in English signs, so when Robby and I worked up enough courage to venture into our bath, I was able to assure him that there would not be any girls in there.

First we went into a kind of locker room, where we took off our clothes and were issued towels and washcloths. Then we went into another area where we sat on little wooden buckets and washed ourselves with soap and water. (A very important rule of Japanese bath-taking is that you clean yourself *before* you get into the bath, because generally you're sharing the bathwater with other people, and they do not wish to soak in your dissolved bodily scum, thank you very much.)

Then it was time to go into the bath area. Robby elected to wear a bathing suit, but I was stark naked, except for my washcloth. Thus attired, we entered the bath area, which was nothing

DAVE BARRY
DOES JAPAN

---

[5] I mean you switch *baths.* You stay the same gender.

like anything I had ever seen on my home planet.[6] The baths were in a vast, high-ceilinged, brightly lit, water-filled room with a sort of island in the middle and neon lights forming giant trees on the walls. There were steaming shallow pools of water all around, some of them the size of swimming pools. Men were soaking in hot baths, medium baths, cold baths, individual-sized baths. There were baths with sand in them, and a bath inside a structure shaped like a bullet train. There were footbridges and water slides. There were . . .

WOMEN! WOMEN IN THE BATHS!!

There were two of them. They were cleaning women. They were about twenty yards away, cleaning, acting as though this was no big deal, being in a bath filled with naked men, although for all I knew they had photographic memories and as soon as they got outside they were going to sit down with police sketch artists and produce anatomically detailed posters for distribution and sale over in the women's bath. So I headed off in the opposite direction, toward a steam cloud, trying to look cool and unconcerned, but walking as though I had suddenly developed a back problem, and holding my washcloth in an unnatural manner.

I cannot say that I ever became totally relaxed in the baths, because the cleaning ladies kept moving, and therefore so did I, hopping quickly from

_____
[6] Earth.

bath to bath, submerging myself quickly, which is
not smart because some of those baths are approximately 17,000 degrees Fahrenheit, which meant I
would emerge nanoseconds later, shooting vertically into the air like a very modest Polaris missile
holding a washcloth over its private parts.

> ### TRAVEL TIP
> If you go to a Japanese public bath, take a *large*
> washcloth.
> Maybe also a wet suit.

After Robby and I left the bath we met up with
Beth, who said that the women's bath was less
stressful but did feature a giant Buddha statue on
the island. As we were discussing this, wearing our
incorrectly tied *yukata,* a group of boys stopped to
stare at us for a while. Finally the oldest one, who
was maybe twelve, said: "How are you?"

"Fine," said Beth. "How are you?"

"Greatness!" said the boy.

We continued to attract attention that evening
when we went bowling. I got the largest shoe they
had, a size "26.0," which apparently refers to the
total capacity of each shoe as measured in foot
molecules. So I was walking funny, but what really
entertained the other bowlers was our bowling
technique. The bowlers around us, after they let go
of their balls, would just *watch* them as they rolled
toward the pins, which struck us as insane, because

of course the real skill in bowling is telling the ball what to do. Hey, the ball *needs* instruction. I mean, during a football game, the coach yells instructions to his players, right? And football players are more intelligent than a bowling ball, right? OK, maybe not, but still, the ball is not a rocket scientist; it's just a ball, which is why we were giving it as much guidance as possible by waving and shouting and assuming helpful bodily postures, much to the amusement of the surrounding bowlers. I thought to myself: Let them laugh. What really matters is the final score, right? And it just so happens that my final score was: Really bad. I blame the shoes.

The next morning we were awakened by an earth tremor. Fortunately it was mild, so we did not have to follow the instruction of the broadcast. Nevertheless it was a disturbing sign, because this was the day when we were going to hell. Actually, we were going to eight "hells," or *jigoku*—hot mineral springs that have long been a tourist attraction in Beppu. We joined an all-Japanese group on a tour bus. Our guide was a woman who walked while holding a yellow flag over her head so we could follow her easily from hell to hell.

Each hell is basically a pool of steaming hot water, reeking of sulfur, sometimes with mud around it. The water burbles up naturally out of the ground, and over the eons the various geological forces involved have resulted in the formation of elaborate gift shops, as well as an Eight-Hell Package Ticket.

Each hell has its own theme: For example, the
Red Hell has red water and a statue of a devil.
Another hell, for no apparent reason, has exotic
animals next to it, including an elephant, lions,
hippos, and turkeys.

Another hell had crocodiles in pens. There
was a sign that said:

> The force of the steam is so strong here that about
> one and a half train cars can be pulled by its
> pressure and it creates ideal conditions for breed-
> ing crocodiles.

This statement is of course based on the well-
known scientific formula relating crocodile-raising
to steam pressure, as measured in freight-car-pull-
ing capacity.

At one of the pens there was a little boy,
maybe four years old, looking down at a large
crocodile. I wandered up and started looking at it,
too, and after a few moments the little boy looked
up at me. His eyes went wide with terror.

"*GAIJIN!*" he shrieked, and ran to his
mother.

Gaijin means "foreigner." To the little boy, I
was scarier than a crocodile.

The exit from each hell took us conveniently
through the gift shop, where we could buy random
souvenirs, as well as specific hell-related items such
as eggs that had been hard-boiled in the mineral
springs. Also for sale was mud, which allegedly had

some value as a medicinal or beauty product. Beth was very impressed with the mud selection and soon was comparison-shopping from hell to hell. For *mud*. Finally she actually *bought* some, and if that doesn't reinforce an unfortunate shopping-related gender stereotype, I don't know what does.

My favorite hell was *Tatumaki Jigoku,* or "Water-Spout Hell." The sign said:

> This is an intermittent spring that forcefully shoots up water to a height of 20 meters every 25 minutes.

And sure enough, it did. We got there about ten minutes before it went off, and we watched the big clock until *boom,* right on schedule the hot water started spouting. It stopped exactly five minutes later, and the crowd went into the convenient gift shop, just as another tour bus pulled up to witness another on-time water-spout performance. How very convenient! Exactly two shows an hour!

I expressed great skepticism about the Water-Spout Hell to Beth. I compared it with Old Faithful geyser in Yellowstone, which is highly reliable, for a geyser, but doesn't operate on anything like this kind of clockwork schedule.

"Yes," Beth said, "but this is a *Japanese* geyser. Efficient! On time!"

I paid her no heed. This is a woman who bought mud.

12

CLIMBING MOUNT FUJI

(Partway)
(In a Bus)
*(At Least We Think
That Was Mount Fuji)*

The last major tourism thing we did in Japan was make the traditional pilgrimage up picturesque Mount Fuji, a dormant volcano, which is defined, geologically, as "a volcano that may not in fact exist."

At least *we* never saw it. It is reputed to be quite large, but we never saw a trace of it the whole time we were in Japan, because it was always covered by a thick layer of picturesque clouds. So although we spent several hundred dollars for a Mount Fuji tour, during which we rode for ten hours in a tour bus that was allegedly driving around, and on, Mount Fuji, all we ever saw, through the dense fog, was the part of Mount Fuji directly below the bus window. It looked a lot like a road. I would say it was dormant.

From time to time, our guide would point out the window and say: "If you look over there, maybe you can just see top of mountain," and we'd all squint into the fog, and if we squinted really hard, we could see something that might have been Mount Fuji. Or it could have been window dirt, or one of those brown things that float around inside your eyeball.[1]

We weren't the only people attempting to enjoy the picturesque beauty of Mount Fuji that day. It was the height of vacation season, and Mount Fuji is one of Japan's most popular destinations. As the guide put it when our bus set out: "Very traffic jam can be expected."

This turned out to be, if anything, a very understatement. As far as we could tell, the entire Japanese nation had been waiting for a day like this, featuring maximum cloud density, to make the Mount Fuji trip.

---

[1] Try not to think about them. They're probably harmless.

So we spent the first few hours grinding slowly along on a car-choked highway, passing the time by eating cookies from a package labeled "Varieties of Bland New Type." The other major entertainment medium on the bus was Brazilians. There was a group of Brazilian tourists on the bus, and they were sociable to the point of mass civil disorder. After three weeks among the Japanese, who tend to be, by American standards, quite reserved, I had come to think of us as quite outgoing and lively and demonstrative; but we are The Night of the Living Dead compared with Brazilians, at least the Brazilians on our bus. They communicated mainly by shouting—happy, vibrant shouts, interspersed with loud laughs and heartfelt emotional greetings, whenever two of them were reunited again after an absence caused by, for example, walking to the other end of the bus.

Their favorite thing to shout was *"Hai!"* This is the Japanese word for "yes," and it appeared to be the only Japanese word that the Brazilians knew. But they *loved* it, and they used it at every available opportunity. The guide, pointing at the fog, would say, "Now maybe you can just see top of mountain," and the Brazilians, not even looking out the window, would shout *"HAI!"* and then collapse with laughter.

Thus we whiled away the hours, inching our way through the traffic to Mount Fuji, then gradually up the slope until we reached the Fifth Station, which is the highest point you can drive to on

Mount Fuji. There we found a very traffic jam indeed. I am quite sure that many of those cars are still up there.

We got out of the bus and wandered for a while in the fog along with thousands of other people. Many of them were hikers on their way to the top, which was a five-hour climb from where we were. It was so crowded that people were waiting in line to get onto the trail, which disappeared up the mountainside, into the gloom. A loudspeaker on a pole constantly blared instructions at the hikers, the noise echoing up and down the slope. I asked our guide what it was saying, and he said, "Mainly it says be careful not to fall down."

Being a bold adventurer who is always ready to take on a physical challenge, I myself set off briskly up the mountain, and I did not rest until about fifteen feet later, where there was a soft-drink vending machine. I would have continued all the way to the top, but our tour itinerary required us to be back on the bus in forty-five minutes, so we could resume sitting in traffic.

One lucky break for us was that there was a large and busy gift shop, which sold every conceivable kind of Mount Fuji souvenir. With an eye toward having something to do on the bus ride home, I bought a nice set of Mount Fuji toenail clippers (the box said "Family Size"). The clerk spent several minutes carefully wrapping the box, as though it were a gift. I hadn't asked him to do this, but by then I was used to it; the Japanese are

big on packaging, and your purchases often get wrapped. (Once, in Tokyo, Robby and I and Tom Reid of the Washington *Post* had purchased desserts in a bakery. Our plan was to take the desserts outside, a distance of maybe ten feet, and eat them, but first the clerk put each dessert into a separate box, which he carefully fastened shut with tape. When we got outside and opened them, we discovered that we were short one plastic spoon, so Tom went back inside to get it. The clerk, who could see that we were eating right outside, nevertheless wrapped the plastic spoon in paper, which he put into a little bag, which he taped shut, before he gave it to Tom. Just doing his job.)

Not that I am complaining about Japanese packaging mania. It was kind of festive, opening my toenail clippers on the bus.

We left the Fifth Station and drove back down the mountain to the popular, by which I mean comically overcrowded, tourist destination of Hakone, where we went to a restaurant. Our group made quite an entrance. There were maybe fifty vacationing Japanese, eating and chatting quietly, and suddenly

HAI!

Fifty heads jerked around simultaneously to see who was shouting "YES!" at them. It was, of course, our Brazilians, whose mood seemed to improve the longer they sat on the bus. They felt better still after consuming a few beers, and soon they were striding around inside the restaurant,

DAVE BARRY doing little dance steps, hurling *hai*s left and right and holding long-distance conversations with each other across the room, over the heads of stunned, staring Japanese, who would not make this kind of noise if they were undergoing surgery without anesthesia. It's probably no accident that Brazil and Japan are located so far apart.

While waiting for the traffic to build up for our return trip to Tokyo, we spent some time in the Hakone area, which is quite pretty and features a spectacular view of the clouds covering Mount Fuji. It also features snack bars where you can buy a popular dish made by frying tiny baby eels until they form a yellowish brown mass of what looks like melted-together spaghetti with zillions of little spots on it. The spots are what's left of the baby eels' eyes. As a bold culinary adventurer I certainly would have tried this dish, but I had to sit down with my head between my legs.

When the traffic was dense enough for our purposes we got back onto the bus and began inching back toward Tokyo. It had been a long day, and eventually even the Brazilians became dormant, as did the rest of us. As night began to fall, I drifted off to sleep listening to the monotonous, reassuring sound of our guide saying that if we looked *now*, maybe we could just see the top of . . .

CONCLUSION

I would say that the single most important conclusion I reached, after having spent three weeks traveling through Japan, as well as countless hours reading, studying, and analyzing this fascinating culture, is that you should always tighten the cap on the shampoo bottle before you put it in your suitcase. Because otherwise—trust me here—it's going to leak all over everything, including your toothbrush, and when you brush your teeth you'll be foaming at the mouth, as though you've been bitten by a dog infected with herbal-scented rabies.

I also discovered that it is possible to gain weight even in a country whose idea of a taste treat is sea urchins.

I'd like to be able to conclude with some deeper insights into the Japanese, but looking back through my notes, I don't find any. I find a lot of notes like: "CORN IN PIZZA!?!"

So I'm afraid that my perspective on Japanese culture was severely limited, similar to the perspective we had of Mount Fuji, riding around in the fog; I was *there,* but all I could see was the tiny bit of it right around me, and even that wasn't very clear. This is my fault. It was stupid of me to go over there without learning to speak at least some Japanese, and I solemnly promised myself to correct this mistake.[1]

When we got back home, the main thing everybody asked was "What was it like?" And I found myself answering, "It was really *foreign.*" I've spent time in a variety of foreign countries, including Miami, and I've never felt so completely, helplessly out of it as I did in Japan. This is largely of course because of the language barrier, especially

---

[1] Of course I was lying.

the written language barrier. In Germany, even if you don't speak the language, you can read the letters, so if you see a typical German sign, like:

Godownenundergroundenpayenfarenridearoundentrainen

You can figure out that this means "subway." Whereas in Japan, most of the time, you're blind. Blind and stupid. And different.

You can never forget for a moment how different you are. Japan is no melting pot. It's an extremely exclusive club, and the only way to get into it is to be born into it, and that's that. We were told repeatedly by Westerners that no matter how long they've lived in Japan, and how well they've learned the language, there remains a fundamental, perceptible barrier between them and their Japanese coworkers and friends. We were always aware of this barrier, much more so than in other countries we've visited. The Japanese always treated us politely; they rarely treated us warmly.

Of course, politeness goes a long way. In fact the thing I liked best about Japan is how *civil* it is. You can walk around in a big city and not get panhandled or hassled or beat up. You can go to a public place and not have to listen to some jerk playing ugly music on a refrigerator-sized, nuclear-powered portable stereo system blasting out sound waves capable of denting sheet metal. You don't find every urban wall and fence disfigured by spray-painting cretins; you don't find vending machines wrecked and pay phones smashed and subway cars pissed in.

You find people respecting each other's property, and respecting each other. It's quite pleasant.

And I still can't get over the service. When you walk into a store or hotel or restaurant, the employees act as though they actually want your business. One afternoon in Kyoto I watched as a car pulled into a gas station; instantly *four* men were working on the car, pumping gas, checking the oil, cleaning the windshield, emptying the ashtray, taking an empty Coke can from the driver. I stayed and watched as another car pulled in, and another, and another; they all got the same treatment. Ordinary customers at an ordinary gas station.

I'm not saying nobody gets this kind of service in the United States. I'm sure it happens routinely to, for example, the president, or Cher. But most of the rest of us, at least if we live in urban areas, endure an enormous amount of lousy service. And rudeness. And hostility. And the threat of random physical violence from strangers. We're used to it. We've learned to protect ourselves by going out into the world with a hard, fuck-you attitude, ready to stomp on other people before they stomp on us.

In Japan, I found myself wondering what it would be like to be Japanese, to live in a society wherein you could automatically assume that you'd receive a certain level of respect and courtesy, even from strangers. Because they aren't really strangers. They're members of your club.

The drawback, of course, is that the club has a lot of rules, strict rules. Wear a uniform, do what you're told, don't be a wild card, don't make waves. The nail that sticks up gets pounded down, that's what Japanese children are taught. Different is bad.

This is a good philosophy if you want to crank out defect-free cars, but it's not so good if you want a diverse, dynamic culture. The feeling I got was that the Japanese are bored with their ritualized, traditional, superrestrictive culture; that's why they so eagerly embrace Western movies, TV shows, music. We Americans have a troubled, chaotic, friction-filled society, but it's never boring. The Japanese may be ahead of us in some areas of technology, but they're a long way from being able to produce, for example, James Brown.

Which is not to say that Japan isn't still a little scary. The Japanese are hard workers and relentless competitors. At times they've made us look bad, and we're not used to that. But I think, in the end, the competition is teaching us an important lesson, which is that just being American isn't enough; we have to work hard, too. American cars are a *lot* better now than they were ten years ago. Does anybody really believe that Chevrolet and Ford and Chrysler would be busting their butts to please us today if it weren't for Toyota and Nissan and Subaru?

Japan isn't our enemy. That notion is racist and stupid. Japan had nothing to do with creating

CONCLUSION our monster national debt, or wrecking our cities, or dumbing down our schools, or making so many of us hate and fear each other. We don't need any outside threats to mess up this country; we're doing fine on our own. And if we're going to solve our problems, we could probably stand to take a few lessons from the Japanese, about things like respect and responsibility.

And the Japanese could stand to lighten up.

In other words, nobody's perfect.

ABOUT THE AUTHOR

"The funniest man in America" said *The New York Times,* in one of their rare bursts of good humor, agreeing with the Pulitzer Prize board, which honored DAVE BARRY with their coveted—especially by Dave—award in 1988 for Distinguished Commentary. ("Even though," said *Newsweek,* "he loves to deflate the *Times*'s pomposity" and "one of his entries razzed the Pulitzers.")

He claims to have gone to Pleasantville High School (in a suburb just beyond New York) and Haverford College (just beyond Philadelphia) and to have graduated both times (beyond comprehension). Afterward, he launched into a career in journalism, narrowly missing the Watergate story to concentrate on West Chester, PA's sewage problems, and soon there was spirited bidding for his talents in the wider world. The *Miami Herald* won, as did Tribune Media Services, which syndicates his weekly column to more than four hundred hapless but happy newspapers.

Dave and his wife, Beth, and their son, Robby, lived for a time outside Miami until Dave, realizing that Miami is not Philadelphia or New York, moved into the city itself.